The Morning Star
JOURNAL

Vol. 15   No. 3

D1301092

Editor: Rick Joyner
Contributing Editors: Jack Deere, Francis Frangipane, Dudley Hall
Managing Editor: Deborah Joyner Johnson
Project Manager: Dana Zondory
Layout and Design: Dana Zondory
Copy Editors: Suzanne Hirt, Tracey Selvey, and Deborah Williams

The Morning Star Journal® USPS012-903 is published quarterly, 4 issues per year, by MorningStar Publications, Inc. A division of MorningStar Fellowship Church, P.O. Box 440, Wilkesboro, NC 28697. Summer 2005 issue. Periodicals postage rates paid at North Wilkesboro, NC and additional mailing offices. CPC Agreement #1472593. ISSN# 10832122

POSTMASTER: Send address corrections to *The Morning Star Journal®*, P.O. Box 440, Wilkesboro, NC 28697

Subscription rates: One year $16.95; Outside U.S. $24.95 USD.

MorningStar Publications is a non-profit organization dedicated to the promulgation of important teachings and timely prophetic messages to the church. We also attempt to promote interchange between the different streams and denominations in the body of Christ.

To receive a subscription to *The Morning Star Journal®*, send payment along with your name and address to *MorningStar Publications*, P.O. Box 440, Wilkesboro, NC 28697, (336) 651-2400 (1-800-542-0278—Credit Card Orders Only); fax (336) 651-2430. One year (4 quarterly issues) U.S. $16.95; Outside U.S. $24.95 USD. Prices are subject to change without notice.

Reprints—Photocopies of any part of the contents of this publication may be made freely. However, to re-typeset information, permission must be requested in writing from *MorningStar Publications Department*, P.O. Box 440, Wilkesboro, NC 28697

BIOS

Francis Frangipane is the senior pastor of River of Life Ministries in Cedar Rapids, Iowa, and the president of Advancing Church Ministries. The Lord has used Francis to unite thousands of pastors in prayer in hundreds of cities. With more than a million copies of his best selling books in print, and with an expanding radio and television ministry called "In Christ's Image," Francis is in much demand worldwide. His newest book is entitled, *This Day We Fight!*

Steve Thompson is the associate director of MorningStar Fellowship Church, and he oversees the prophetic ministries for all of the MorningStar Fellowships. A gifted teacher and prophetic minister, Steve travels extensively throughout the United States and abroad as a conference speaker. Steve's newest book, *A 20ᵗʰ Century Apostle, The Life of Alfred Garr*, was released through MorningStar. Steve and his wife, Angie, reside in North Carolina with their five children: Jon, Josh, Madison, Moriah, and Olivia.

Tom Hardiman is the director of the MorningStar Fellowship of Ministries and MorningStar Fellowship of Churches. He is a former church planter and pastor, with more than twenty-five years of experience in ministry. Tom has a heart to help serve and mentor the emerging generation of pastors and church leaders. He and his wife, Mary Anne, live in Charlotte, North Carolina with their three children.

Lloyd Phillips, director of Fellow Laborers' International Network (FLInt Net), is committed to equipping the saints for Christian service. Traveling and teaching for more than twenty-five years in the United States and abroad, Lloyd seeks to establish God's divine order within the church and work with others to "both do and teach." Contact info: FLInt Net, P.O. Box 113, Missoula, MT 59806. Phone (406) 251-8580, Fax: (406) 251-7035, e-mail: flintnet@flintnet.org. Website: www.flintnet.org.

John Paul Jackson is the founder and chairman of Streams Ministries International located in North Sutton, New Hampshire. A popular teacher and conference speaker, John Paul travels around the world teaching on prophetic gifts, dreams, visions, and the realm of the supernatural. His newest publication, *Moments With God Dream Journal*, offers a unique approach to dream recording. To order his books and tapes, please call 1-888-441-8080, or visit his website at www.streamsministries.com.

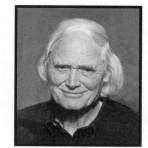

Geri Keller, a reformed church pastor, and his wife Lilo, lead the "Stiftung Schleife" ministry in Winterthur, Switzerland.. Their ministry mandate is to equip the saints by hosting conferences and seminars, as well as providing prayer and counseling opportunities for leaders and pastors.

Christie Wills is originally from southern Minnesota, and she studied at Bethel University in St. Paul, Minnesota before moving to Charlotte to attend MorningStar School of Ministry. She is a graduate of the first year program at MSM, and is currently in school to finish her degree as a registered nurse. Christie has a heart for healing and has done mission work in both Costa Rica and India. She and her husband, Jacob, reside in North Carolina.

Mike Roberts is originally from the Charlotte, North Carolina area and has been involved at MorningStar for about ten years. He is a graduate of the MorningStar School of Ministry, and has a heart for the prophetic ministry and teaching. Mike is currently on staff at MorningStar Publications and Ministries and lives in Moravian Falls, North Carolina.

Rick Joyner is the founder, executive director, and senior pastor of MorningStar Fellowship Church. Rick is a well-known author of more than thirty books, including, *The Torch and the Sword,* the long awaited sequel to *The Final Quest* and *The Call,* and his latest, *Delivered From Evil.* He also oversees MorningStar's School of Ministry, Fellowship of Ministries, and Fellowship of Churches. Rick and his wife, Julie, live in North Carolina with their five children: Anna, Aaryn, Amber, Ben, and Sam.

Robin McMillan is currently pastoring the MorningStar Fellowship Church at our H.I.M. facilities near Charlotte, North Carolina. With a unique preaching style, prophetic giftings, and a desire for the release of God's power, many are impacted by Robin's ministry. Robin and his wife, Donna, live in North Carolina and have four children: John Mark, Christopher, Andy, and Katy.

BIOS

Matt Peterson is the director of the MorningStar School of Ministry located at our H.I.M. facilities near Charlotte and the pastor of the MorningStar Fellowship Church in Winston-Salem, North Carolina. Matt and his wife, Debbie, have five sons: Josiah, Seth, Sam, John, and Andrew.

Tom Archer is a former Marine Corps pilot and graduate of the U.S. Naval Test Pilot School and now serves as the chief test pilot for the FAA in Seattle. In addition to leading a staff of test pilots and aerospace engineers, he regularly tests a variety of jet transports and helicopters. He has traveled extensively in the United States and overseas. Tom and his wife, Jackie, are members of MFM, and have two daughters and two grandchildren.

Deborah Joyner Johnson is the managing editor of the Publications Department and oversees all publishing projects for MorningStar Publications and Ministries. She shares with her brother, Rick Joyner, a desire to see the body of Christ provided with the highest quality spiritual food that is relevant for our times. Deborah's second book, *Pathway to Purpose*, was recently released through MorningStar. She has a gifted teaching ministry and shares at conferences and women's groups. Deborah lives in North Carolina and has three children: Matthew, Meredith, and Abby.

Lilo Keller and her husband, Geri, lead the ministry of "Stiftung Schleife" and "Schleife Publications." For more than twenty years, they have pastored several churches in Switzerland and one in Germany. Lilo has recently taken on the executive leadership of the ministry. Lilo, along with her worship team, the "Reithalle Band," travel internationally. As a prophetically gifted songwriter and worship leader, she has produced nine CDs, including her piano solo production *Humming Bird* that was birthed on a sabbatical in Moravian Falls, North Carolina. She and Geri have two sons who are married.

Eric Swisher and his wife, Lorie, have been in worship ministry in southeastern Idaho for thirty years. They are co-founders of a 24-hour worship center, and lead a home church that encourages people to find their hearts and stay on their paths. They enjoy working with Christian musicians and artists in the area, and have just finished a prayer and worship CD, "Things Above." Their family includes three adult children and two grandchildren. Eric can be reached at swisher@ida.net.

WALKING IN ETERNAL LIFE

by Francis Frangipane

God's end-time people will "end time." What I mean is that, as we near the end of the age, we will increasingly learn how to walk in eternal life, abiding above the boundaries, constraints, and the pressures of the realm of time. We will see what's coming and either avoid it or announce it, but we will not be limited by it.

Jesus taught that those who come to Him **"have everlasting life"** (see John 3:16). Right now, we have eternal life in our spirits. Yet, how do we access the timeless place of God's presence? This is a serious question, for we have become more "time conscious" than "God conscious." Schedules, meetings, appointments, and deadlines all fuel our anxieties and compel us to live horizontally instead of vertically in the presence of God. The Lord seeks to deliver us from anxiety, but this can only happen if we truly learn to walk in the Holy Spirit. The sad fact is, most Christians fail to spend time with the Holy Spirit. We pray, even calling upon the Lord, but few have cultivated moment by moment openness to the Spirit of God.

"But, when He, the Spirit of truth, comes, He will guide you into all the truth; for He will not speak on His own initiative, but whatever He hears, He will speak; and He will disclose to you what is to come" (John 16:13).

The Holy Spirit **"will guide...He will speak...He will disclose"** to us what we otherwise could never know or attain. To guide, speak, and reveal are forms of communication. Clearly, the Father sent the Holy Spirit to talk to us.

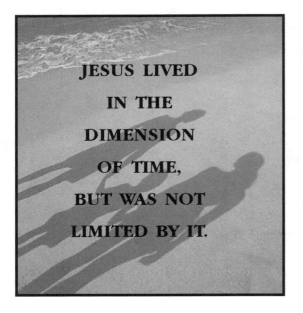

JESUS LIVED IN THE DIMENSION OF TIME, BUT WAS NOT LIMITED BY IT.

The Holy Spirit is the Spirit of Truth. There are issues in our hearts that the Holy Spirit alone can reveal and remove. Listen to Him. Like Christ, He does not come to condemn but to save. His voice is salvation speaking to us.

Jeremiah said that the heart is deceitful above all things (see Jeremiah 17:9). We cannot objectively know ourselves. Yet the Holy Spirit, who is the Spirit of Truth, sees and understands our ways. Trust Him; He cannot be deceived. Indeed, the ancient Greeks used the same word for truth as they did for "reality." Thus, we could accurately say that the Holy Spirit is the "Spirit of Reality." He shows us the reality of our need and the reality

of God's answer. To hear Him is to hear the voice of eternal life.

Jesus lived in union with the Holy Spirit continually. The miracles He accomplished came through the power of the Holy Spirit. Through the Spirit He saw the things the Father was doing; He heard the Words the Father was speaking. Every strategy we may come up with pales in comparison to seeing God, doing what He does, hearing Him, and saying what God says. You see, Jesus lived in the dimension of time, but was not limited by it. His consciousness was always aware of the eternal realm.

Even the urgent news of Lazarus' illness did not make Jesus move anxiously. As right as it seemed to rush to Lazarus' aid, Jesus was aware of another reality. He was conscious of the heavenly Father. Because He knew that the Father was about to raise Lazarus from the dead, He lived without hand-wringing or being driven by anxious thoughts or pressures.

Oh how we need to walk in the Spirit today. In every situation, we would consciously be aware of God's involvement in our lives!

"For My thoughts are not your thoughts, neither are your ways My ways," declares the Lord.

"For as the heavens are higher than the earth, so are My ways higher than your ways, and My thoughts than your thoughts" (Isaiah 55:8-9).

God has a system of thoughts and ways that are totally on another plane, yet He invites us to abide with Him! Beloved, we are not mere human beings. We are each a temple for the Holy Spirit, but we must cultivate a listening heart if we will do the things that God is doing. A Christian is not just someone living out a natural life, hoping that God will bless him. No, God has more for us than that. Jesus set the standard, and He's given us the Holy Spirit so we can follow Him.

Spirit Filled?

When we are born again, we begin a journey with the Holy Spirit. The Spirit gives us gifts to help us grow; He baptizes us in power to increase our effectiveness. All of this is to lead us until we are actually filled with the Holy Spirit, where we think and act like Jesus.

Many of us think we are already filled with the Spirit, but we are not. We have three quarts of self and one quart of the Holy Spirit, and we think we have a gallon of God. There is still too much self-ruling in our hearts. In America, some pastors identify themselves as being Spirit-filled and say they pastor Spirit-filled churches. To be perfectly candid, I have never attended a church that is truly Spirit-filled. In the book of Acts, we see a picture of a Spirit-filled church. The leaders met daily for prayer, and on the way to prayer, their shadows healed the sick! Their offerings went to feed the poor. Out of their sense of love and community, they held all things in common. In that atmosphere, the church grew exponentially.

I know some are thinking, "My church is getting close to this example." Oh, I forgot to mention, in a Spirit-filled church, if you lied, you died (see Acts 5:1-6).

Let's not accept that we are further along spiritually than we are. God desires to take us further and deeper into eternal life. Being born again and having a spiritual gift does not mean that you are filled with the Holy Spirit. I have never met a true spiritually mature person who was anxious; no one who is nervous about time can truly be led by the Holy Spirit.

Where Do We Go from Here?

In our quest to walk in eternal life, we must allow the Holy Spirit to excavate self from our hearts. If we want to tune into the God channel, we must tune out the "self channel," where the anxieties, fears, and sins exist.

I want a heart that can hear God; I want perception that can see God. We are too much like the world. How do we break this? Spend time with the Holy Spirit. Ask Him to talk to your heart and then write down what you feel He is saying. If we want more of God, we must cultivate the awareness of His Presence, and especially listen for His voice.

We must also take faith and believe that the Spirit is here to help. Zechariah 4:6 teaches us that it is not by our might or power, but it is by the Spirit of the Lord that we succeed. Acts 2:17 tells us that in the last days God seeks to pour out His Spirit upon all flesh. I love the words "pour out." We must stop thinking trickle and think Niagara Falls!

It is time to step out of the box called "time," and live in the Spirit. I'm not suggesting that you become unreliable or be late for your appointments, but that you give yourself to learning how to hear God's voice and how to live in His presence. If you are one of God's end-time elect, then it is time to rise above the pressures of time and walk in the eternal life of God. ∎

The Purpose Of PROSPERITY

by Steve Thompson

God wants to prosper you. He wants to break the spirit of poverty over your life and release significant financial resources to you. But there are several deeper issues to be considered with this promise.

First, God desires more than simply blessing us personally. He wants to release resources for establishing His kingdom on the earth. Second, He does not want prosperity to dampen our desire for Him and spiritual things. Last, He is giving us an opportunity for faithfulness with natural resources so we can be trusted with **"the true riches"** (see Luke 16:11).

Money provides tremendous opportunities, but also brings difficult tests. In fact, with the remarkable material prosperity released in our generation, "being blessed" has proven a curse for many people. When their money and material possessions have increased, many solid Christians have tragically lost their heart for God and the furthering of His kingdom.

Many of these failed when tested with financial blessing because of three mistakes. First, they largely misunderstood the purpose of financial increase and money in general. Second, many did not embrace the repentance that John the Baptist preached. Third, when God released prosperity to them, they allowed their focus to drift away from Him and toward the natural wealth He had provided.

The Purpose of Prosperity

There are many misunderstandings about prosperity floating through the church today. The extremes are obvious—some believe God wants every believer poor so we will be completely dependent on Him. On the opposite end, others believe God wants to make everyone wealthy beyond their imagination so we can live life in ease and comfort. The truth lies somewhere between these two extremes.

GOD BLESSES US SO WE CAN BLESS OTHERS FOR HIS KINGDOM.

Without elaborating in great detail, the reality is God wants to prosper His people as we embrace the principles outlined throughout the Scriptures. He wants us to be diligent in work, wise in investments, sober in our spending habits, and faithful in our giving. In other words, God's plan for blessing His people is based upon our adherence to the wisdom outlined in His Word. Get rich quick schemes are denounced by the Scriptures.

Understanding that God wants to prosper us and the pathway to prosperity is important. However, we also need to recognize the pitfalls of prosperity or we may discover too late that we have fallen into them. Proverbs 1:32 states, **"...the prosperity of fools shall destroy them"** (KJV). Only a fool would want

financial wealth or natural resources without the wisdom to use them properly.

Money or material prosperity is not simply provided as a personal reward from God for obeying His will. While it is a foundational concept that God's blessing follows our dedication to sound principles of life and business, there are more profound and nobler reasons that God releases wealth to His people.

Although He loves and wants to bless us, God does not provide wealth simply so we can enjoy it. This fallacy stems from the selfish perspective plaguing much of our contemporary Christianity. God has a deeper desire in blessing us materially. His hope is that we embrace the joy of participating with Him in extending these blessings to others by giving. In other words, God blesses us so we can bless others for His kingdom.

Resources Not Just Blessings

It is God that gives you power to gain wealth that He might establish His covenant on the earth (see Deuteronomy 8:18). God releases money and other material resources to those who are faithful in His kingdom. Their service may have been in any arena, not just financial. However, because of their faithfulness and obedience within these different arenas, God provides additional resources to them, including money. But the increase they experience should be understood as kingdom resources, not just personal rewards or blessings.

Because this concept has been so fundamentally misunderstood, any increase in prosperity has often brought about complacency in believers by revealing a profound selfishness within them. Instead of recognizing that they received a greater stewardship, many thought they were simply being blessed for their faithful service. With this self-centered perspective, they began to consume through their lusts the resources they were supposed to extend to others.

GOD WANTS TO BLESS US SO THAT OUR NEEDS ARE COMPLETELY COVERED IN EVERY AREA AND WE HAVE AN ABUNDANCE TO GIVE CHARITABLY TO EVERY GOOD WORK.

God does want to bless us, and we should understand that, but His intentions go beyond blessing us. According to II Corinthians 9:8, **"God is able to make all grace abound to you, that always having all sufficiency in everything, you may have an abundance for every good deed."** God wants to bless us so that our needs are completely covered in every area and we have an abundance to give charitably to every good work.

However, based on much self-centered theology, many instead believe God gives to us so that *we have an abundance of every good thing.* The pivotal misunderstanding here revolves around the purpose of money. Money, along with other resources, is given by God to provide for us and our families, and so we can do good in His name and further His kingdom on the earth.

We Cannot Avoid the Test

Some believers have understood the potential that money has to corrupt them and therefore seek to avoid dealing with financial increase. Although this is a noble intention, running away from prosperity is not part of God's plan for dealing righteously with it. Money, like all resources, is necessary and needed for doing His will. It is our own wrong desire for having money, born of selfishness that is an issue.

When God provides us with greater material resources to use for His kingdom, we must embrace these resources gratefully, but soberly. We must overcome the temptation to build for ourselves instead of releasing to others. If we pass this test, we find an amazing opportunity to grow in God's nature and character, which is based on giving.

There is a significant temptation when provided with material blessing to move away from our devotion to spiritual principles. And this is a crucial test of the validity of our faith. We must grow in faith and devotion to God while increasing in material wealth or will we fall to trusting in the temporal instead of the spiritual.

Historically, many have failed this test. They lost their "faith walk" when finances increased. They subtly began trusting in their wealth instead of the Lord when any increase came. It is well-documented within Western society that as income increases, the percentage people give away actually shrinks, and this includes Christians. However, this does not have to be repeated in our lives. We can live differently if we make better choices, based on a better understanding.

> **THE ISSUE BEFORE US IS HOW TO RECEIVE MATERIAL WEALTH FROM GOD AND USE IT FOR HIS KINGDOM, INSTEAD OF SIMPLY CONSUMING IT ON OURSELVES.**

Jesus declared that it was impossible to serve both God and mammon (see Matthew 6:24). So the issue before us is how to receive material wealth from God and use it for His kingdom, instead of simply consuming it on ourselves. We must also discover how to experience an increase in our devotion to God and His kingdom while experiencing increase in the material realm. Last, we must discover God's plan for how we can redeem material blessings for greater spiritual authority and power.

The Repentance We Need

The first answer for us is found in repentance—not just our contemporary ideas of repentance, but biblical repentance. When John the Baptist burst onto the scene, his message was simply, "*The kingdom of heaven is at hand. Repent so you can enter it.*" The message is simple—to enter or experience the kingdom of heaven, we must repent. But what are the practical steps of repentance required of us?

This was the same question the people posed to John after coming to his baptism and hearing him preach repentance. Remarkably, his answers to three different groups asking this same question had one theme—overcome your love of money and your trust in material possessions. We find this exchange in Luke:

To the multitudes John said:

"Let the man who has two tunics share with him who has none; and let him who has food do likewise (Luke 3:11).

To the tax collectors John answered:

"Collect no more than what you have been ordered to" (Luke 3:13).

To the soldiers John said:

"Do not take money from anyone by force, or accuse anyone falsely, and be content with your wages" (Luke 3:14).

John's answer to everyone was: Stop trusting in material possessions. He then made it even more practical for them by giving specific directions. Be content with your pay scale. Do not try to gain financially by cheating another person. Do not put your faith in money or material blessings. Trust God to provide for you as you look out for others.

JESUS WAS SAYING WE CANNOT SERVE BOTH GOD AND THE DESIRE TO BE FILLED TO FULLNESS WITH WORLDLY, TEMPORAL POSSESSIONS.

These were profoundly simple steps of repentance, but in each case they dealt with a heart attitude toward money or possessions. This repentance or turning away from our trust in money and natural provision is necessary for us to experience the kingdom of heaven.

Our heart must become unfettered by the love of money or material blessings, or we will fall and not ascend higher as God desires. The issue is learning that we are called as conduits of blessing, not their end point. Paul quoted Jesus in Acts 20:35 as saying, **"It is more blessed to give than to receive."** God wants us to have

so we can give, not just have so we can be full.

Who Do We Love?

The desire for fullness really is the issue. When Jesus stated that it was impossible to serve God and mammon, He was not just denouncing money (see Matthew 6:24). Mammon is not just another expression for money or material resource. Mammon was actually a demon deity of *fullness* worshiped by pagan cultures. Jesus was saying we cannot serve both God and the desire to be filled to fullness with worldly, temporal possessions.

Jesus was warning us of the power of mammon. We must understand that mammon has power, and we must continually wage warfare against the control it seeks over our lives. Do not be deceived; we cannot serve God and mammon. We cannot place our security in being full of this world's provision and serve God at the same time.

Practically though, how can we know if we trust God and love Him, or if we trust in money and love it? One way love is revealed is by our reaction to the proximity of the object of our affection. How do you feel when God is close to you? Do you feel secure and protected, empowered and joyful? When He appears to be distant, are you despondent and helpless?

What about our reaction to money and provision? When we have money or provision, do we feel better, empowered, protected, and secure? Are we forlorn, fearful, and depressed when it is distant? When money goes away from us, are we depressed? Can we say with Paul that we have learned to be content in all states, abounding or being abased, or do we love money so much that we have lost our need for God? Getting our heart straight about money and our attitude toward it is crucial for our generation.

Choosing Poverty of Spirit

There are practical ways to avoid setting our affections on money or temporal things. If we intentionally live with an open hand as John the Baptist prescribed, we wage a constant warfare against this temptation. Additionally, we can make structured choices to increase our standard of giving, not our standard of living, as God blesses us materially. By doing this we acknowledge our position as stewards of His resources, not just consumers of His blessings.

Additionally, while God wants to break the spirit of poverty off the church, we must in turn embrace poverty of spirit. While the phrase "poverty of spirit" is arcane, the sentiment it represents is sorely needed today. Poverty of spirit or being poor in spirit means *to know our need for God*.

Being poor in spirit or recognizing our need for God is our best protection from the corrupting influence of money and material blessing. If we know our need for God and grow in our pursuit of Him, it will protect us against selfishly using financial increase that God extends for

our stewardship. Otherwise we will fall to living only according to the kingdom of this world.

Jesus said that the kingdom of heaven belongs to those who are poor in spirit (see Matthew 5:3). In other words, when we know our need for God, it enables us to rise above the temptations to only accept a worldly or earthly kingdom. If we can walk out the repentance John preached, even when financial increase or material prosperity comes, we can experience the kingdom of heaven.

> WE CAN MAKE STRUCTURED CHOICES TO INCREASE OUR STANDARD OF GIVING, NOT OUR STANDARD OF LIVING, AS GOD BLESSES US MATERIALLY.

In this way, material blessings do not have to be an impediment to walking in the kingdom of heaven. In fact, part of God's plan for releasing financial resources is to provide us a pathway for experiencing a more spiritual, supernatural realm. Financial resources can provide an amazing springboard for moving in greater realms of spiritual authority and power, if we respond correctly when they come.

The True Riches

Jesus hinted at the hidden potential of properly stewarding material resources in a parable He told His disciples. In Luke 16 Jesus tells of a steward who was unfaithful with His master's possessions. He then made this statement as an application:

"He who is faithful in a very little thing is faithful also in much; and he who is unrighteous in a very little thing is unrighteous also in much.

"If therefore you have not been faithful in the use of unrighteous mammon, who will entrust the true riches to you?" (Luke 16:10-11).

There is something available to us that Jesus describes as **"true riches"** when compared with unrighteous mammon. The pathway to being entrusted with these true riches, in part, is properly stewarding the natural resources that God extends to us. Financial blessings, when stewarded wisely, provide pathways to true riches. The true riches God wants to release to us are spiritual authority and supernatural power to demonstrate the kingdom of God.

God wants to release to us amazing authority over sickness and disease. He wants to release profound authority over demonic influences that oppress mankind. He longs to release the miraculous to His people. Amazingly, one way He does this is by giving us natural resources to teach us faithfulness, and to grant us access into the kingdom of heaven.

Redeeming the Natural for the Supernatural

When God entrusts us with natural resources, this presents us with an amazing opportunity to experience spiritual power and authority. Another way of saying this is that the natural resources are redeemable for supernatural resources. God will actually enable us to give our natural resources and gain heavenly access as a result.

THE TRUE RICHES GOD WANTS TO RELEASE TO US ARE SPIRITUAL AUTHORITY AND SUPERNATURAL POWER TO DEMONSTRATE THE KINGDOM OF GOD.

Years ago, just after graduating from the university and before I was married, the Lord instructed me to give all of my money to a couple who were expecting their first child. Although I had a specific need personally, the Lord told me that He wanted to pay for this child's birth and His plan was to use my money to do it. He reminded me of how often I told Him that all my possessions belonged to Him, and now He wanted to discover if I really believed it.

This was a significant test for me. I had a specific impending need for the money. It actually took several hours of dedicated prayer before I found strength to obey—partially because the Lord revealed that my need would go unmet for four months. Later that evening, as I gave the money to this couple at the Lord's direction, I discovered it fully covered their expenses. Also, as the Lord had spoken, my own needs were not met for more than four months after this.

Eight years later, while I was praying with a group of pastors, the Lord spoke to me in a stunning fashion, *"I will provide whatever you ask of Me for your children, as long as you live."* I was caught off guard because I was praying for the pastors gathered, not my two sons. The Lord continued, *"Because you paid for the birth of that child eight years ago when I asked you to, I will do whatever you ask Me for your own children."* I was overwhelmed when I realized the implications of my obedience many years before.

God had allowed me to redeem unrighteous mammon for supernatural provision without even realizing it. My obedience in giving at the Lord's direction opened a reservoir of supernatural resources for my children beyond anything I could imagine.

Over the years, as my family has grown to include three daughters in addition to my two sons, I have marveled as God has quickly and repeatedly answered my prayers for them. They have experienced supernatural healings, vivid dreams from God, remarkable prophetic giftings, and a deep commitment to righteousness. I thank God frequently for asking me to give sacrificially many years ago. I now realize that when God asks for something, He is trying to bless us, not take something away.

> MY OBEDIENCE IN GIVING AT THE LORD'S DIRECTION OPENED A RESERVOIR OF SUPERNATURAL RESOURCES FOR MY CHILDREN…

This is the foundation of covenant relationships. When two people are in a covenant relationship—they have agreed that all they possess belongs to the other. God has brought us into this type of covenant relationship. The way that He allows us to access this covenant is by asking us to give what we have at His direction. If we have demonstrated faith by releasing whatever He asks, He in turn will give us access to whatever He has that we need. We effectively trade our natural resources for His supernatural resources.

We need to understand that when God asks us for something, He is looking to bless us, in addition to others. Every act of obedience toward God opens something profound to us in the kingdom of heaven. However, because of our unrenewed minds, we see most things wrongly. God wants to bless us, not harm us, by encouraging us to give freely to others. If we will obey His voice and release our material possessions at His instruction, we can redeem them for supernatural realities that are much more precious. We can really experience the kingdom of heaven, if we know our need for Him, and not just natural things.

The Laodicean Opportunity

In Revelation 3 we find a remarkable situation with the Laodicean Church. This church was devoid of passion for Jesus and spiritual realities. Their fall had occurred because their affection was centered on their wealth and abundance instead of God. Jesus described them as being neither hot nor cold—which are both supernatural states, but as lukewarm which is the natural state of all things. Called to be a supernatural people, they were most decidedly natural in all ways.

"Because you say, 'I am rich, and have become wealthy, and have need of nothing,' and you do not know that you are wretched and miserable and poor and blind and naked,

"I advise you to buy from Me gold refined by fire, that you may become rich, and white garments, that you may clothe yourself, and that the shame of your nakedness may not be revealed; and eye salve to anoint

your eyes, that you may see" (Revelation 3:17-18).

Because their focus was on material wealth, the Laodiceans were no longer poor in spirit. They actually believed they had need of nothing— including the Lord, who later revealed that He stood on the outside of this church. Though they had remarkable material blessings, they were spiritually bankrupt and were currently living only in the worldly realm, with no access to the kingdom of heaven.

WE CAN REALLY EXPERIENCE THE KINGDOM OF HEAVEN, IF WE KNOW OUR NEED FOR HIM, AND NOT JUST NATURAL THINGS.

However, even though their state was so pitiful and perilous, Jesus gave them the greatest promises of any of the churches in the Revelation. Consider the opportunity He extended to those who repented and overcame.

"...be zealous therefore, and repent.

"Behold I stand at the door and knock; if anyone hears My

voice and opens the door, I will come in to him, and will dine with him, and he with Me.

"He who overcomes, I will grant to him to sit down with Me on My throne, as I also overcame and sat down with My Father on His throne" (Revelation 3:19-21).

These are remarkable promises. Although they had abandoned the pursuit of Him for natural things, Jesus promised this church that He would come and have intimate fellowship with them. He also promised to elevate them to sit with Him on His throne. In other words, Jesus offered to grant profound spiritual authority—the right to sit with Him on His throne, to those who overcame their fallen focus on being increased and full.

Jesus extended these remarkable promises to those who heard His voice and opened the door for Him. We must hear the Lord's voice calling us to return to a life as stewards of His resources instead of consumers of His blessings. And we must open the door for Him, by obeying His instruction to extend these resources to others as He directs. If we are zealous in this repentance, the results will be astounding.

We will experience intimate fellowship with Him and experience a more full spiritual authority than we can now imagine. We must choose poverty of spirit and continue seeking the Lord, redeeming the natural blessings for supernatural realities. The purpose of prosperity is to use it wisely to open the doors of the kingdom of heaven. ■

The greatest good you can do for another
is not just share your riches,
but reveal to them their own.

—Benjamin Disraeli

≫≫≫ Mustard Seeds of Wisdom ≪≪≪

OUR COMMUNION OF SAINTS

All Scriptures are New King James Version.

by Tom Hardiman

The recording of the Last Supper in the Gospels imparts a powerful illustration of fellowship. These records give us an inside view of some very personal exchanges which occurred throughout the evening as Jesus met with His disciples. They teach us much about what the Lord intends for us when we gather in communion.

The Greek word for communion is *koinonia*. When we examine this word more closely, it communicates very desirable qualities. This word conveys the idea of partnership, common purpose, and of course, fellowship.

Partnership

Partners are individuals who work in close cooperation and communication with each other. Partnership, at its best, implies an open and honest dialogue wrapped in the warmth of friendship.

As we observe the interaction surrounding the Last Supper, Jesus displayed an unmistakable love, respect, and concern for His friends. During the meal, He revealed treasured secrets to His closest associates. He approached them in humility and washed their feet. He commanded them to love one another and prayed for their unity. Above all, Jesus sought to ensure that they were well-prepared for His departure. He treated them as true partners in His kingdom. In turn, the disciples also evidenced genuine warmth and care for Jesus, and for other members of the group.

We must remember that Jesus shared this partnership with flawed men. Even while the Passover meal was being eaten, character flaws manifested around the table. An argument about who would be the greatest raised the tension level at the table, and then Peter demonstrated spiritual blindness when he adamantly stated that he would never deny Jesus. But in spite of these obvious deficiencies, Jesus continued to express love for His friends. God's greatest demonstration of His power of salvation and deliverance is preceded by a powerful expression of partnership with common men who will carry on His purposes.

Common Purpose

Communion also proclaims our common purpose. When we unite around a common purpose, great things happen. The history of Israel demonstrates this. Prior to David becoming king, the tribes of Israel were harassed by many enemies. But then something extraordinary happened. **"All these men of war, who could keep ranks, came to Hebron with a loyal heart, to make David king over all Israel; and all the rest of Israel were of one mind to make David king" (I Chronicles 12:38).** When they united to make David their king, their ability to defeat their enemies multiplied. From that point, Israel's history

changed and they became a dominant force in the region.

In the same way, when one hundred twenty people gathered together in one accord on Pentecost, they witnessed a powerful demonstration of the Holy Spirit. They then began to turn the world upside down as three thousand were added to the church that day. Unity of heart and a common purpose released an unprecedented time of advancement as God's Spirit moved freely among His people.

Fellowship

When we join together in mutual love and cooperation, the kingdom will advance. True fellowship is coming. It will change the church. The body of believers will practice true love, concern, and care for each other. True fellowship provokes a response from the unsaved. They know we are Christians when we love each other.

Satan will not sit back passively while the church moves toward this destiny. He will attempt to sow discord, isolate individuals from the body, and target the stragglers, the weary, and the tired. Moses recognized this part of Satan's strategy when he spoke to Israel: **"Remember what Amalek did to you on the way as you were coming out of Egypt, how he met you on the way and attacked your rear ranks, all the stragglers at your rear, when you were tired and weary; and he did not fear God" (Deuteronomy 25:17-18).**

Satan's strategy has not changed. He recognizes that when he separates people from the body, they are more prone to excess, imbalance, and moral failure. And woe to that man who is alone when he falls; for who will pick him up? (see Ecclesiastes 4:9-10).

GOD HAS PLACED US TOGETHER SO THAT WE MIGHT DRAW UPON OUR COMPANIONS FOR NEEDED PERSPECTIVE, WISDOM, AND STRATEGY.

We all must remember the exhortation of the book of Hebrews, **"And let us consider one another in order to stir up love and good works, not forsaking the assembling of ourselves together, as is the manner of some, but exhorting one another, and so much the more as you see the Day approaching" (Hebrews 10:24-25).** God has placed us together so that we might draw upon our companions for needed perspective, wisdom, and strategy.

Communion is more than a ritual, it is a Christian lifestyle. We must give high priority to establishing, building, and developing relationships with partnerships formed, common purposes forged, and fellowship fortified. Let us participate in this communion as often as we can. ■

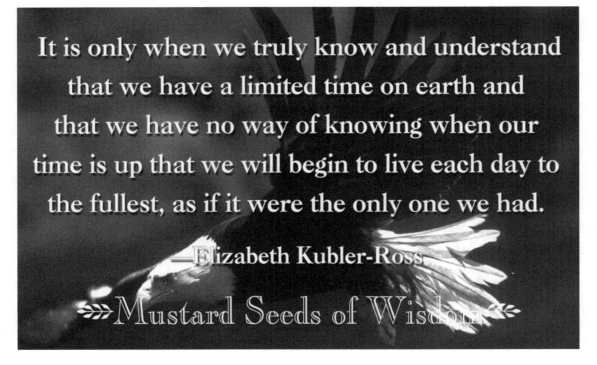

It is only when we truly know and understand that we have a limited time on earth and that we have no way of knowing when our time is up that we will begin to live each day to the fullest, as if it were the only one we had.

—Elizabeth Kubler-Ross

≫≫ Mustard Seeds of Wisdom ≪≪

TEAM UP THE HORSES

All Scriptures are New King James Version.

by Lloyd Phillips

There is something about spiritual fathering that is like training horses from out of the flock of God. Many of us do not have a vision of the church that goes beyond a flock of sheep. We envision the flock will follow the voice of the Shepherd and depend upon Him to be led to water and pasture. But there is something inherent in spiritual fatherhood that has the authority and mandate to raise up warriors to do battle for the Lord.

The spirit of Elijah is prophesied in Scripture as that spirit which restores spiritual fatherhood to the people of God (see Malachi 4:5-6). When Elijah was taken up, Elisha, his spiritual son, took up his fallen mantle in a figure of succession. As Elijah rose up in the whirlwind, Elisha cried out **"My father, my father, the chariot of Israel and its horsemen!" (II Kings 2:12).** While there is a pastoral anointing to gather and guard the flock of God, there is an anointing of spiritual fatherhood which raises up horsemen and chariots to do battle for the Lord.

Breaking Self-will

I began to receive prophetic direction and insight a number of years ago regarding raising up horses from among the sheep. This represents raising up the people of God into their God-given gifts and callings of service in the kingdom. Not being a horseman or cowboy by trade or training, I was dependent upon others to teach me what is necessary in training horses. It became clear, even from a cursory look, that there is much to be learned about raising up the saints of God into ministry from the stages of training up horses to be useful for service.

Most everyone is familiar with the term "broken" as applied to horses that have been worked with for some time. A horse that is not broken cannot be ridden, nor is it useful for any form of service. Likewise a horse that has a broken spirit will obey only what it is directly led to do and no more. It ceases to think on its own. The idea is to break the self-will of the horse, but not his spirit. Consider the similarity to people who function with a broken spirit (see Proverbs 18:14). However, if we, as the people of God, will allow ourselves to be broken upon the Rock in humility, then we are at a place where the Lord can begin to train us up. If we remain self-willed, we are like the un-broken horse which must be left out to pasture, serving no useful purpose to its master.

> **It is the actual struggle to become free from the cocoon that strengthens the butterfly, giving it the ability to eventually fly away and fulfill its purpose.**

One way of breaking the stubbornness of a horse is to simply tie it to a post while it is a colt or a yearling. The colt will not like the strange feeling of being tied to a post. The post is strange, as is the rope, and the sense of loss of freedom may well be the worst feeling the colt has ever experienced. A wise trainer will not give the colt too much rope; he will give him enough to pull back on, but not enough so that the colt can rear back, flip over, and get hurt. A wise trainer will give a student enough rope to learn, but not enough to "hang himself."

I was told the following story by a woman who has trained many horses in her life. As a child she had a particularly pretty yearling which she especially favored. It was quite spirited, and when it was tied to the post it really struggled and tried to get free. She knew she needed to leave that colt tied to the post until it was through struggling, but she had sympathy for it and released it prematurely. In so doing, she ruined the horse. It could not be broken and eventually was sold.

There is a well-known story about a man who was watching a butterfly emerge from its cocoon. He had compassion for the butterfly as it struggled to be free of the cocoon and at times seemed exhausted. It appeared as though the butterfly would never be able to emerge. So the man decided to carefully help release it from the cocoon, thus ending the struggle. He was surprised when, after a time, the butterfly did not fly away upon beautifully colored wings. Instead the butterfly remained with shriveled wings and eventually died without ever being able to take off. He later found out that it is the actual struggle to become free from the cocoon that strengthens the butterfly, giving it the ability to eventually fly away and fulfill its purpose.

Likewise, when the yearling was loosed from its struggle prematurely, it created a mind-set within the colt which it was never able to overcome. Perhaps Jesus was referring to this same struggle when He spoke to Saul as he traveled to

Damascus with the words, **"It is hard for you to kick against the goads" (Acts 26:14).** I can recall many images in my memory from the television westerns where the rider dismounts from his trusty steed at the hitching post only to loosely drop the reins over the post and walk away, never once expecting that his horse wouldn't be waiting for him when he returned. This was only possible because the horse was broken and therefore was trusted and obedient.

Learning to Wait

Provided in the Gospel of Luke is a relevant parable for those being equipped for service to the Lord. Jesus said:

> **"Go into the village opposite you, where as you enter you will find a colt tied, on which no one has ever sat. Loose it and bring it here.**
>
> **And if anyone asks you, 'Why are you loosing it?' thus you shall say to him, 'Because the Lord has need of it.'"**
>
> **Then they brought him to Jesus. And they threw their own clothes on the colt, and they set Jesus on him.**
>
> **And as He went, many spread their clothes on the road (Luke 19:30-31, 35-36).**

The Lord sent His disciples to find a colt that had never been ridden, and yet had been broken by view of the fact that he was tied to a post but was not fighting. This represents the type of person that is not self-willed, but has remained at his post until he is called. When a soldier is given an assignment, he is expected to remain at his post for the specified time or until relieved. Too often those with self-will remaining in their hearts do not have the patience to remain at their posts, leaving before they are summoned. How many potential ministers have missed their calling through impatience, feeling that they have been overlooked or neglected? Rather than wait to be summoned, they wandered away from the post before they could be called out. It is one thing to be "chomping at the bit" in excitement and anticipation, but quite another to wander away from the post. The Bible promises us that if we will wait, we will be strong, mount up, and run.

Too often those with self-will remaining in their hearts do not have the patience to remain at their posts, leaving before they are summoned.

But those who wait on the LORD shall renew their strength; they shall mount up with wings like eagles, they shall run and not be weary, they shall walk and not faint (Isaiah 40:31).

The colt in Luke was not impatient but had become used to the post and was eventually brought before the Lord. He did not present himself, but was presented by another. When Joseph brought his two sons, Ephraim and Manasseh before his father for a blessing, they each received a full reward, more than they could have received by presenting themselves (see Genesis 48). Fatherhood opens the door for a double blessing.

Blessings of the Father

Once the disciples presented the colt to the Lord, something interesting happened—it states the apostles laid their clothes upon the colt. This is a symbol of the protective covering that comes to those who are in proper arrangement with godly leadership. There is a covering which comes supernaturally to those who will remain at their post and follow where they are led. But that is not the end of the parable, the Lord sat upon the colt. This represents the Lord's anointing coming to sit upon the ministry of the person being raised up. Just as the Lord Himself received the Father's blessing in a voice from heaven after the Spirit sat upon Him, likewise when a person is raised in submission and obedience, the Lord's anointing will abide upon him and the blessings of the Father will remain.

Another important aspect of this analogy is after the Lord sat upon the colt the Bible states, **"as He went, many spread their clothes on the road"** **(Luke 18:36).** In other words, the people received Him. There is no guarantee that a minister who has "loosed" himself into ministry will be received into the congregation of the Lord. There is something

illegitimate about ministry which is loosed prematurely and without relational covering. There are so many gifted individuals who know they have a call from God, but are frustrated about not being received into the assembly of the people of the Lord. Deuteronomy 23:2 may give us some insight into the reason: **"One of illegitimate birth shall not enter the assembly of the LORD; even to the tenth generation none of his descendants shall enter the assembly of the LORD."** There is something about a ministry which is birthed or released prematurely or illegitimately that makes it difficult for the assembly of the Lord to receive. Illegitimacy is the result of improper fathering or the absence of a father. The heart of fatherhood is able to restore those who are wandering to the point where they may be received into the congregation of the Lord.

Train Up the Spirited

There must also be understanding on the part of the trainer as to the difference between a spirited horse and one that is not coachable. I once heard Rick Joyner address a meeting of pastors and leaders concerning training up the saints of God. He pointed out that it was easier to work with geldings than it was to work with stallions because stallions have more will and spirit. He pointed out that too many pastors had neutered their young men in an attempt to exercise control. However, a gelding cannot produce offspring, so, if we are truly interested in raising up future generations to the Lord, we, as leaders, need to work with and train up the spirited horses without removing their ability to reproduce. They may sometimes fight and quarrel much like the disciples did, however, when all is said and done, they will produce fruit that will remain.

The Round Corral

Another very interesting aspect of horse training occurs in a round corral. As opposed to a regular corral, which is used for holding stock and may have corners, the round corral has no corners for a young horse to get backed into. It is important when training a horse not to allow the horse to become cornered, but to allow it to move around and around as many times as it takes until the task which is being taught is accomplished.

Horse trainers know that it is in the round corral where an understanding and a bond of real trust are acquired. One very interesting attribute which is imparted during the time in the round corral is the trust that the horse builds with its trainer that encourages the horse to respond to the trainer's voice. An untrained horse, or one that has not been worked with sufficiently, will need to be corralled or lassoed. Those that have been trained in the round corral where trust is built will come when called and allow themselves to be bridled and saddled for a day's work or a ride. This is the principle we see recorded in Psalms 32:9, **"Do not be like the horse or like the mule, which have no understanding, which must be harnessed with bit and bridle, else they will not come near you."**

The wisdom learned in the round corral is applicable to working with people. We must be willing to allow people to go around and around as many times as it takes until they get it right. If our systems allow for corners where people can get backed up or hide, then they may not expend sufficient energy to conquer the task at hand properly. What initially seems uncomfortable and strange to the horse will actually come in very handy to the horse in the future. From the center of the round corral, the trainer does not need to chase the horse down as it runs around again and again, but can simply reach out from the center position and encourage it either to go back around and try again, or praise it for accomplishing the desired behavior.

A Higher Platform

I recently watched as a horse trainer worked with a young horse attempting to teach it to step up onto a platform which was about one foot high off the ground. The platform at first caused the horse to become alarmed, as it had not experienced anything that looked quite like the platform before. As the horse approached the platform it would come to a stop while it checked out the unfamiliar object. The trainer had a long crop with a plastic bag tied on the end which would make a ruffling sound when it was shaken in the air. When the horse would stop at the platform, the trainer would calmly praise the horse and encourage her to step onto the platform. When the horse became uncomfortable, she would go around it and the trainer would hold out the crop and shake the bag behind her to keep her running around the corral until she returned to the platform. This process was repeated many times over. I was surprised that it only took about ten minutes before the horse first placed one hoof on the platform. On the next try she placed both hooves on the platform. At this point the horse seemed to actually enjoy the view from a higher vantage point.

Equipping the Saints as a Team

Understanding comes with time, experience, and relationship. Equipping the saints is more complex than simply training a horse to obey, but it is like training a horse to be teamed up with other horses. The principle of "one can chase a thousand, two can chase ten thousand" is as apparent with teaming up horses as it is with raising up saints who can work as teams for the good of the kingdom. A team of horses can pull more than ten times as much as two horses could working independently. This is also true with raising up believers as laborers for the harvest. Too often we assume that a person is fully trained when he is equipped to accomplish the things which he has been trained to do at an effective level. I do not believe that the job is complete at this point. It seems more powerful to impart the clear ability for the horses of the Lord's chariot to be yoked *together* for the good of all. Ephesians 4:12 does not say the ascension ministries are to equip a saint but to equip *the saints*—plural.

The perfecting of the saints for works of service must be seen as incomplete until they are serving as a team. The words of the preacher from Ecclesiastes 4:9 are: **"Two are better than one, because they have a good reward for their labor."** As the saints are raised up into service as ministers of the gospel, it is important to realize the multiplied benefits of being teamed up together for the work of the ministry. We must certainly be able to pull our own load, but the kingdom is enhanced when we learn to pull together. We must work to *Team Up the Horses* for the chariot of the Lord so that the kingdom is revealed according to the plan of the Lord. ■

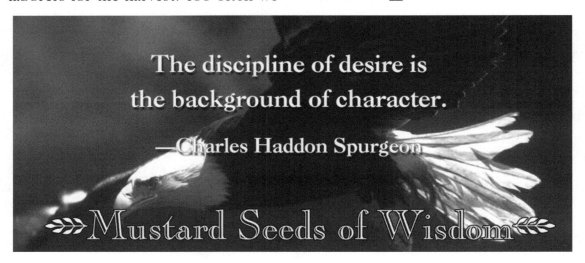

The discipline of desire is
the background of character.

—Charles Haddon Spurgeon

≫ Mustard Seeds of Wisdom ≪

The Importance of Building CHARACTER

All Scriptures are New King James Version unless otherwise indicated.

by John Paul Jackson

It takes people with godly character and habits to effectively serve in God's kingdom. While there are many talented and anointed leaders, those who have a foundation of godly character (moral excellence) lead more than by their words. They lead by their lifestyle in ways that are truly transformational. It is just as important what we tell others, as who we are as we minister. It is who we are, more than what we know, that inspires change in another person's life.

We must decide to take the necessary steps to strengthen our own moral legacy. Leaders must practice what they preach. They must realize that moral excellence can only be built through Bible study, quiet times with God, and a history of making right choices—what I call "hidden victories." These hidden victories ensure long-term success in the kingdom.

Sadly, character is a topic the church often pays lip service to, but rarely teaches people how to walk in it. All of us can remember examples of people who were put into positions of leadership based on their anointing and gifting, but they lacked character. We also remember the disheartening results. Such leaders had great charisma and great anointing, but like Samson their moral deficiencies brought their demise.

When leaders have a gift that is greater than their character, stress and anxiety is generated. Such individuals feel the pressure to perform and succeed. They have a reputation they feel must be maintained. Deep inside they are afraid to let God do the work of advancement and recognition of their ministry and calling, so they begin to rush ahead of God and promote themselves before they are truly matured by God.

Four Components of Character

As I have studied Scripture and meditated on God's perspective about character, I have concluded that there are four components that evidence healthy, godly character: love, integrity, maturity, and an abundance mentality.

Love is essential to every ministry. The Apostle Paul made this clear when he wrote this stunning sentence: **"If I speak God's Word with power, revealing all his mysteries and making everything plain as day, and if I have faith that says to a mountain, 'Jump,' and it jumps, but I don't love, I'm nothing"** **(I Corinthians 13:2 The Message).** What a statement!

Throughout God's kingdom, there have been generations of what I call "gifted nothings"—people who have done miraculous work, but who never truly understood the need for intimacy with God and the love of Christ. No wonder love is the first fruit of the Holy Spirit listed in Galatians 5! Love must be evident in our lives.

Integrity is the act of being entirely honest at all times. Leaders must forge a foundation of trust with those whom they are mentoring, equipping, and leading. If a leader has integrity, his or her lessons will be remembered, because people will have seen the leader's actions match his or her words.

Jesus had the highest level of integrity possible; His disciples knew He practiced what He preached. This inspired them to strive to be like Jesus, both in word and deed.

Maturity involves sound reasoning and decision-making. When a person has walked through the fiery trials and difficulties of life, spiritual maturity is developed.

> **IT TAKES THE PRIVATE TESTING OF GOD TO SEE A PERSON'S CHARACTER SOLIDIFY AND MATURE.**

God says in Isaiah 48:10, **"Behold, I have refined you, but not as silver; I have tested you in the furnace of affliction."** This furnace is at full flame when we are off the platform, living our lives away from the public eye. It takes the private testing of God to see a person's character solidify and mature.

The result of maturity is meekness, which is how we interact with others. Maturity allows us to esteem others higher than ourselves. Maturity allows us to see God's plan in our chaos.

An abundance mentality sees God as having so much talent and anointing to give people that no one person has a corner on the market. Embracing an abundance mentality requires that we demonstrate humility. It is not about us anyway; it is about God and His kingdom. Anything less allows jealousy to manifest in our lives. We must have a heart that blesses the gifts others have, knowing that all gifts are given by God to help others and to further advance God's kingdom on earth.

Who Are You When No One Is Watching?

We cannot become truly great in God's kingdom unless we walk through adversity, pain, and difficulty. Joseph was made second-in-command of Egypt after years of wrongful imprisonment and unfair slavery. Gideon delivered the Israelites from their enemies after struggling with insecurity and fear. Samuel left his parents and served in the often-lonely temple before growing into a great prophet and judge. David became a beloved king after years of living in caves and dodging death threats. Paul was blinded and then persecuted as his ministry grew. These private battles forged great leaders of God.

Likewise in the daily grind of life, hidden victories form a foundation for how we will operate publicly.

What do we do when no one is watching us?

How do we treat our spouse?

Are we devoting quality time with our children?

Are we respectful of our co-workers?

Are we being generous financially and spiritually?

Have we overcome the issues of rejection and fear that have plagued our lives?

Have we restored broken relationships?

Are we speaking and praying blessings over others?

> **WE CANNOT BECOME TRULY GREAT IN GOD'S KINGDOM UNLESS WE WALK THROUGH ADVERSITY, PAIN, AND DIFFICULTY.**

It takes hundreds of these seemingly insignificant hidden victories to form a solid foundation of character upon which God places the weightiness of public ministry.

When David wanted to face Goliath, he told Saul about his private victories: **"Your servant has killed both lion and bear; and this uncircumcised Philistine will be like one of them, seeing he has defied the armies of the living God" (I Samuel 17:36).**

David's history of hidden victories as a shepherd gave him the faith and confidence to face Goliath publicly as a protector of Israel's future. A foundation of character, formed humbly and quietly in the hidden moments of life, had been built in the future king's life. Little did David know how these events would allow God to use him one day. As we overcome our personal battles, God can trust us in a deeply spiritual way in ministering to others.

Listening for the Holy Spirit's Heartbeat

I believe we are tripartite human beings. We are comprised of three parts: body, which is flesh, bone, and blood; soul, which is our mind, will, and emotions; and spirit, which is the source of wisdom, communion, and conscience.

All ministry—teaching, mentoring, discipling, and leading others—flows from one of the three parts of our being. The challenge for prophetic individuals is to listen carefully to the Holy Spirit's heartbeat. We must continually be sensitive to listening to the Spirit and to cleaning out the issues that keep our soul in the driver's seat of our lives. We must turn ourselves over to the work of God's Spirit and develop a history of hidden victories.

It takes discipline and practice to fully understand the distinction between what is our own soul and what is the leading of the Holy Spirit. We must be committed to allowing more and more of His essence to flow through us.

We must develop ever-growing, godly character and walk in greater integrity and maturity. Only the Lord, by helping us practice our private victories, can make our lives a lasting and public contribution to His eternal kingdom. Only then can we help others reach the exciting destiny God created for them. ■

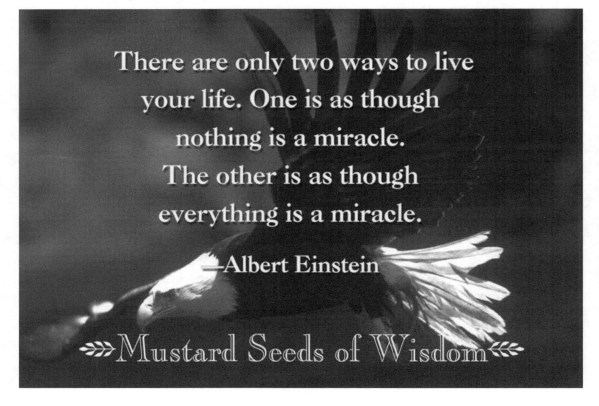

There are only two ways to live your life. One is as though nothing is a miracle. The other is as though everything is a miracle.

—Albert Einstein

≫≫ Mustard Seeds of Wisdom ≪≪

Holy Ground

All Scripture is New International Version.

by Geri Keller

The first statement in the Apostles' Creed declares, "I believe in God the Father Almighty, Maker of heaven and earth." It has to be that way. The Apostles' Creed must start with us entering the realm of the Creator God. Whoever consciously enters the realm of creation with an open heart—be it the starry sky in the quiet of the night or the first light at sunrise—will get a sense of it. This is a very special realm, *holy ground*, compelling us to take off our shoes. That, rather than knowledge, is the prerequisite for ministry; in order to encounter God we need to enter such a holy realm.

That is what the story of Job is all about. His three friends waited seven days before they started to argue what might have caused the plagues and the terrible disasters that destroyed all his possessions and killed his sons and daughters in a single moment. However, they never really entered into a *realm of silence*. They merely waited seven days until they finally stepped behind the pulpit and dumped on Job their elaborate messages— everything they had recollected from their numerous lectures and seminars. Job himself jumped into the argument without entering into the realm of silence. As the story unfolds, God becomes the first one to reveal Himself by entering into that awesome realm of silence, the realm of creation, the domain of the Creator's heart. In doing so, He revealed to Job and his friends the glory of His creation. In the end, Job declares, "I repent in dust and ashes. I spoke of things I did not understand, things too wonderful for me to know. But now I plead, Lord, please instruct me" (adapted from Job 42:1-6).

Geri Keller   31

The Realm of Silence

For the same reason, Moses had to ascend upon Mount Sinai in order to meet God: **"When Moses went up on the mountain, the cloud covered it, and the glory of the LORD settled on Mount Sinai. For six days the cloud covered the mountain, and on the seventh day the LORD called to Moses from within the cloud. To the Israelites the glory of the LORD looked like a consuming fire on top of the mountain. Then Moses entered the cloud as he went on up the mountain. And he stayed on the mountain forty days and forty nights"** (Exodus 24:15-18).

We need to enter into that realm of silence if we are to encounter God and hear from Him. Even Jesus with His three disciples went up to Mount Tabor, the so-called Mount of Transfiguration, because this was the only place where He could get a full panoramic view of the Father's heart. We see the same in the book of Revelation. When the seals are broken, the vast spheres of heaven and earth open before us. As we enter, we sense that these are not just words and powerful images—it is the sphere of God!

At old-time cattle markets, before consenting to purchase cows, smart merchants would have them stand in one spot for a couple of hours to give the cows ample time to pass water accumulated in their bodies. The same happens to us when we enter into the realm of God— the Father, Son, and Holy Spirit. There needs to be a time of purification and emptying of the waters that keep rising to our heads.

The "Seven Days"

God established the period of preparation to last for seven days. Seven, the number of completion, is also the customary number for the Levite ministry. Aaron and his sons, who were anointed to be priests, were given the following directive, **"You must stay at the entrance to the Tent of Meeting day and night for seven days and do what the LORD requires…"** (Leviticus 8:35).

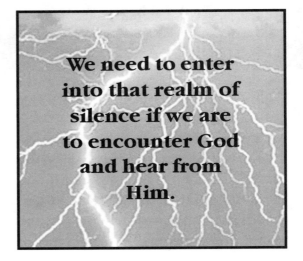

We need to enter into that realm of silence if we are to encounter God and hear from Him.

The seven days Israel had to silently march around Jericho were a means of bringing them into the realm of God. Once we are in that realm, we hear the mockeries of those standing on top of the city walls making fun of the army marching in silence. "Before you go ahead and raise the battle cry, before you start putting your clever strategies into practice, you need to enter the realm of silence for seven days. Then you'll raise the battle cry!" (see Joshua 6:1-5)

The prophets knew this very well. When they received a dream or a word, they usually did not go ahead and proclaim what they had received. Prophets were people who entered into the realm of God first. Therefore, Samuel told Saul: **"Go down ahead of me to Gilgal. I will surely come down to you to sacrifice burnt offerings and fellowship offerings, but you must wait seven days until I come to you and tell you what you are to do" (I Samuel 10:8).** Once again we are confronted with those seven days! Later we read how Saul grew impatient because the people started to scatter. More and more of them started complaining, "Nothing's happening here. Let's go home. There's too much work to do in the fields to just sit around and wait here." Saul obviously did not have a clue as to how to tackle things strategically in the kingdom of God, and felt that this was just a waste of time (see I Samuel 13:8). Nobody really understood that the waiting period was actually the realm of God that the army had to enter first.

It was not about getting the burnt offerings over with as quickly as possible in order to finally go ahead and attack. The seven days were a time of preparation, a time to meet the Lord. When Samuel still did not show up on the seventh day, Saul started taking matters into his own hands and prepared the offering himself. Then, suddenly, Samuel appeared and confronted him, "What have you done? You acted stupidly because you did not obey the command the Lord had given you" (adapted from I Samuel 13:13). His lack of understanding ultimately cost him the kingdom and the victory over his enemies.

The night after His resurrection, Jesus appeared to His disciples. A week later, Jesus appeared once again to meet Thomas. Having missed the first appearance of Jesus, Thomas stated, **"Unless I see the nail marks in his hands and put my finger where the nails were, and put my hand into his side, I will not believe it" (John 20:25).** At this point, having had a real encounter with the risen Lord, Thomas confessed, **"My Lord and my God!" (John 20:28).**

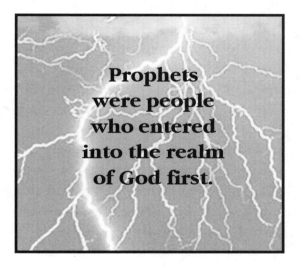

Prophets were people who entered into the realm of God first.

Before we venture out into spiritual warfare, we need to enter into a sphere of silence, the Creator's domain, the holy realm of encounter where we shut the door behind us.

The Realm of Worship

Therefore, Jesus said, "When you pray, go into your inner room and close the door" (adapted from Matthew 6:6). There, in that inner closet, the only room that can be locked, the wide spaces of God will unfold—the realms of the Father, the realms of the anointed One, the Son of Man, the realms of the Spirit! This is where heaven stands open and where angels ascend and descend. Whenever you leave this room, your face will be anointed. Therefore, the worship in our services is not primarily meant to fill up some time, it has a vital function. We worship because we want to enter that realm together as believers, a realm in which our eyes and ears are opened, and we suddenly become aware of the power of the Creator, the power of Jesus and of His blood, and the power of the Spirit.

When our brothers and sisters on the worship team travel, they sometimes spend four hours in worship, and to them, the time just seems to fly because they enter into that holy realm where God speaks to them. They sense that they are standing on holy ground, a place where you feel compelled to take off your shoes. Whenever we come in touch with that realm, we realize that we are unable to do our work without it.

Patience

Patience is a fruit of the Spirit. The New Testament states twice that we need patience in order to receive the promise (see Hebrews 10:36 and Revelation 13:10). Oftentimes, people cut the green fruits off the tree and put them in the microwave to make them look ripe and tasty. However, these fruits will never taste right. This is not the way God does things. We need patience in order to receive the promise, not fake apples for display and artificial food to sustain our people.

At Schleife Ministries, we still do not quite understand what it means to be "apostolic," or "prophetic," or what an apostolic, prophetic lifestyle really is. We are seeking Jesus and the Holy Spirit, and we are longing for the Lord to extend His grace to the "fellowship of saints" that is gathered here because we are so very hungry and thirsty! Our prayer is, "Lord, here we are. Reveal Yourself to us." Jesus promised that He would reveal Himself to those who belong to Him. We are taking Him up on His Word that says, **"Draw near to God and He will draw near to you" (James 4:8 NKJV).**

...without patience we will miss the hour of our visitation; without patience we will not be able to bear fruit for eternity.

Without patience, we will miss the kingdom of God; without patience our moments of breakthrough will not bear lasting fruit; without patience we will miss the hour of our visitation; without patience we will not be able to bear fruit for eternity. As the Scripture says, we need patience! This statement has nothing to do with sitting around and twiddling our thumbs, it means that we are giving the Spirit room to birth things.

I received a postcard showing a tree that was deeply and securely rooted in the ground. Written on the card were the following words, "When a tree is born, it won't be fully grown right away. When it is grown, it won't blossom right away. When it blossoms it won't bear fruit right away. When it bears fruit, the fruit won't ripen right away. When the fruit is ripe, it won't be eaten right away." That is an awesome illustration. At the bottom of the card, it said: "Patience."

A Room of Preparation

These are the ways of the Lord. In the end, the ways of the Lord will yield victory. They are glorious. They provide for us the breakthrough we have been promised. The nations will belong to our God, but only if we enter the realm of silence. It is a realm of awe where we are being prepared and tested. God wants to know whether we are really serious. God does not speak according to our expectations, but He sovereignly speaks whenever He wants to. We will never be able to contain Him. Therefore, let's learn to become ever more sensitive to His voice. But even an increased sensitivity will not spare us the patient waiting, even if we happen to be the greatest prophets.

There are many lessons to be learned in the waiting loop that will ultimately enable us to see true breakthroughs, but it takes patience! We do not know when the Lord will come, when He will speak to us out of the cloud. The cloud first and foremost represents the fact that we are unable to hear, see, or sense a thing. However, God promised that our cup would overflow (see Psalms 23:5).

Our God, the **"I am who I am" (Exodus 3:14),** is so awesome that we have to meet Him, simply because He is God, not just in order to be fit for His service. Our God was able to create a whole world in an instant and He could sovereignly do it again any time. It is by His grace that He decides to involve us rather than doing things all by Himself. Yes, it is our destiny to share in His power and to rule with Him, but He by no means depends on us!

Standing Before God

It seems like the situation in Israel is stuck in a deadlock, in spite of all the political maneuvering. The Oslo Peace Process is dead and the Roadmap also seems to be dead. From a human point of view we seem to be at the end of our rope. However, God is waiting for people to enter into the realm of silence. He waits for Rabbis, Orthodox Jews, and Messianic Jews to enter together into a time of inner preparation. Recently, Messianic leaders went on a retreat together with Arab Christian leaders in the desert in order to enter the realm of God's presence. If there is to be change in Israel, it certainly will not come through discussions among experts—it will only come when people enter the realm of God once again. That is the place where we stand before God, just like Moses did, while his people—

those millions of men and women, elderly, children, infants, and livestock waited in the desert. Down in the plains they built the golden calf, but Moses stood before his God. The question is: Are we standing before God?

Authority Gained in the Realm of Silence

Many of us have been in the ministry for years, some for decades. Some are intercessors, watchmen on the walls, and some have a degree of authority that makes demons tremble. Through others healing is flowing, healing which comes from the wounds of Jesus. Some have an apostolic mandate; others are called to be prophets. We are like racehorses, ready to take the kingdom of God. Yet, my prayer is that in spite of the eagerness, in spite of all our big visions and authority that is given to us, God would grant us the grace to humble ourselves under His mighty hand and to wait in the cloud in order to meet our God, Creator, Father, Brother, Friend, and Lord Jesus Christ in the midst of it.

I want to see men and women, young and old, emerge from the cloud standing like trees planted on the banks of a river—trees like the cedars of Lebanon that are mentioned in the Psalms—trees to lean on, trees that stand tall through times of drought. Jeremiah mentions trees that have **"no worries in a year of drought" (Jeremiah 17:8)** because their roots go deep.

These people are familiar with the realm of silence. They know the Creator God with His hail, wind, lightning, fire,

and devastation. They also know the Creator God who creates life and a new world out of those things. They know this realm, and therefore they have deep roots.

> ...we should be guided by a sense of peace that transcends all understanding, enabling us to "rest from our own works..."

Our hallmark is an attitude of peace, calmness, and serenity! Our hearts are full of passion, but this passion should not be a false fire, a misguided zeal. Above all we should be guided by a sense of peace that transcends all understanding, enabling us to "rest from our own works," from our jealousy, our selfish ambitions, and the notion that we need to accomplish things in our own strength. The kingdom of God must be solidly established in our own hearts. **"The kingdom of God is within you" (Luke 17:21).** It is within us and it is immovable.

The world may be turned upside down, circumstances around us may turn as hot as a boiling cauldron, the media may confront us with one catastrophe after the other, but **"the One enthroned in heaven laughs; the Lord scoffs at them" (Psalm 2:4),** and **"You are my**

Son; today I have become your Father" (verse 7), the Messiah, the Anointed One. God is looking for people who are willing to leave behind all the noise to withdraw to the realm of silence and who will later take the radiance from that realm back into their everyday lives, wherever they are, whatever function they fill. We will get to know Him deeper and deeper as we enter into the holy realm, learning to wait for "seven days."

We are to take that radiance back into the world—the radiance of the Creator, the radiance of our God who says about Himself, "I am the God of patience and consolation" (adapted from Romans 15:5). Our God is full of patience. In fact, He Himself *is* patience. He brought forth creation; He will bring forth the new heaven and the new earth; apostolic and prophetic people will arise—men and women, children, youth, and elderly who will be rulers in this world where more and more nations are becoming increasingly difficult to govern. Our God is asking: "Where are My sons and My daughters?"

They will emerge from the Oval Office of silence, endowed with an authority, a radiance of peace, determination, the shield of faith, and the double-edged sword of the Spirit, right from the mouth of Jesus. By God's grace, they will turn the tides. ■

We must either draw nigh to men
and so draw away from God,
or draw nigh to God and away
from men. The choice, though
not easy, is always ours.

— Leonard Ravenhill

⋙ Mustard Seeds of Wisdom ⋘

All Scriptures are New International Version.

by Christie Wills

Weariness is engraved in our eyes and on our faces. It feels like a part of our DNA. We never quite define it, but instead hint at its existence with words like "I'm so stressed out" or "I have so much to do that I never get a break." We spend our days, evenings, weekends, and holidays working, driving, socializing, volunteering, learning, achieving, doing more and more, yet feeling increasingly overwhelmed with the nagging feeling that we have not done enough.

It seems from infancy we are programmed to believe that faithfulness to the Lord and success in the spiritual and the natural are products of packing our schedules to involve every good and noble cause. The dawn of technology has promised us convenience and efficiency,

luring us with the possibility that we can achieve to an even greater measure. In return, we have sacrificed quietness and simplicity for pressure and noise, faster deadlines, later bedtimes, and another list of things that should have been done yesterday.

In the clamor of our lives, the Lord still calls to us. **"In repentance and rest is your salvation, in quietness and trust is your strength" (Isaiah 30:15).** Yet, we find ourselves wondering where we will find the time for this rest. Even if we manage to sit for a moment, will we be able to rest our minds to enjoy His presence and hear His voice? Or has achieving the presence of the Lord become another demand on our already packed agendas?

Throughout the past months, I have found brief moments to stop and contemplate the state of my own life, only to realize that I have become the archetype of the overbooked Christian. I have joked at times that my headshot should appear next to the definition of "busy" in the dictionary.

I admit that I have spent days running from school to work, to a second job, to a friend's house, and finally back home late at night, never once stopping to enjoy the Lord. I have answered multiple voicemails in the car while driving to my next activity, yelled at stoplights when they did not turn green fast enough to fit my schedule, and steamed internally at the thought of waiting in a five-minute line at the grocery store. I have attempted to have a "quiet time" in the Word while simultaneously eating breakfast, reading my e-mail, and checking my daily calendar as my cell phone rings noisily in the background. Somehow, this all seems to take the "quiet" out of the quiet time. Is this the Lord's best?

In a society plagued by chronic overactivity, it is natural to question, "What is rest?" *Webster's Dictionary* defines rest as "a freedom from activity or labor; a peace of mind or spirit." Rest is stillness in our minds and stillness in our bodies. A common predicament among overbooked Christians is the ability to become physically still without becoming mentally still. Even when our bodies pause, our minds continue to run. It is amazing to think that one brain, measuring around

fifteen centimeters high, can hold an entire memory, a set of emotions, feelings, thoughts, opinions, and seemingly never desire a short hiatus. It is bizarre that we must coerce our minds to slow down.

> BELIEVING THAT WE CAN IS SIMPLY SELF-FOCUS, AN ATTITUDE THAT CAN NEVER BRING PEACE OR REST BECAUSE IT IS ROOTED IN THE SIN OF PRIDE.

Yet, it is in this slowing down process that we become free from ourselves in order to focus instead on the Lord. Constantly running minds and bodies create anxiety, worry, and stress because we become focused on our own abilities or lack thereof. We become particularly stressed when we realize that our own strength will never be enough to complete the tasks at hand. Yet, we have never been called to do anything without the Lord. Believing that we can is simply self-focus, an attitude that can never bring peace or rest because it is rooted in the sin of pride.

True rest and peace is confidence in our salvation, confidence in the Lord's provision for us, and confidence that we are approved by the Lord without regard to what we have or have not accomplished. We know we have achieved this rest when we look forward to our time of listening to His voice, hearing the Lord easily without being rushed, and feeling no guilt for tarrying with Him as long as He calls us to stay.

IN A STATE OF BUSYNESS AND STRESS, ATTAINING REST WILL BE A CHOICE AND A SACRIFICE.

The Lord's call for this season, I believe, is to bring each of us into a place of biblical rest with Him. In this place the Lord becomes our first priority, and we are able to drop everything at any moment to hear His voice. In this place we are also free from the striving mentality that causes us to do more and more in a vain attempt to gain the favor of the Lord or the praise of others. We are free to do only the things that He has called us to do, reserving time for rest and communion with Him.

The next question is, naturally: "How do we attain such biblical rest?" Biblical rest will not come easy. In a state of busyness and stress, attaining rest will be a choice and a sacrifice. It will be a choice to prefer the Lord over ourselves,

to sacrifice our need for praise from others, and to discipline our minds and bodies to slow down.

A few years ago, a friend of mine from Minnesota was diagnosed with lymphoma, a type of cancer that attacks the lymphatic system. He spent months upon months in hospital beds, too weak to do much of anything at all while enduring excruciating treatments. At several points, his immune system became so weak that the number of visitors allowed to see him was limited by medical order. It seemed like the lowest point in his life.

Finally, after multiple rounds of chemotherapy and much prayer, his body became free from cancer cells and he was able to return home. He was asked about his time in the hospital, and we expected to hear horrifying stories about the illness, the medications, the isolation, and the pain. Instead, I remember being rather surprised by his response. He told us how thankful he was for the entire experience of illness, and also, of course, for his healing. Why? While he was ill he had learned to rest, and thus, he had experienced the Lord in an entirely new way.

Hopefully, for most of us it will not take such a dramatic experience to teach us rest or return our focus to the Lord. In fact, in this season, I believe that the Lord will be drawing us each individually into this place when we submit ourselves fully to Him. As I have sought the Lord for personal revelation on the area of rest, He has spoken to me about the keys for allowing Him to transform my life. These keys may also be helpful to you in your journey toward a restful life in Jesus.

Recentering

Recentering is simply coming back to the place where Christ is at the center of our entire lives. Philippians 3:7-8 says, **"But whatever was to my profit I now consider loss for the sake of Christ. What is more, I consider everything a loss compared to the surpassing greatness of knowing Christ Jesus my Lord, for whose sake I have lost all things. I consider them rubbish that I may gain Christ."** Considering everything loss for the sake of Christ means that Christ is to be our first priority. In other words, nothing else in our lives should be as important as knowing and serving Him. Similarly, nothing should govern or claim us as God does—not a person, thing, idea, hope, or dream.

This concept is easy to talk about but difficult to put into practice. In the twenty-first century, we are bombarded with choices—where to go, what to eat, what to wear, what to be involved in, who to work for, and who to be friends with, just to name a few. Each of these choices clamor endlessly for our time and energy. How can we choose to prefer God? I have found that preferring the Lord above all else is only possible as we begin to recognize His love for us. When we know the depth of His love, we will naturally be drawn to Him and desire to place Him first. Knowing this kind of love requires a new level of intimacy with Him.

Intimacy with Christ

I have learned that it is very possible to spend time in the Word, pray daily, read about the Lord, talk about the Lord, be involved in the church, and yet lack any sense of intimacy with Him. If none of these things will bring us intimacy, how will we achieve it?

MEETING THE LORD IN THE HEAVENS IS AS SIMPLE AS HAVING THE FAITH TO BELIEVE THAT WE ARE ALREADY THERE.

Ephesians 2:6-7 states, **"And God raised us up with Christ and seated us with him in the heavenly realms in Christ Jesus, in order that in the coming ages he might show the incomparable riches of his grace expressed in his kindness to us in Christ Jesus."** As believers, we have free access to the heavenly realm. At any moment of the day, we can commune with the Lord because we are already seated in heavenly places with Him. In fact, our existence in the heavenly realm is more real than our existence on earth. Meeting the Lord in the heavens is as simple as having the faith to believe that we are already there. As we commune with Him, we may see visions, hear His voice, or simply feel a sense of peace in our hearts and spirits. Despite the experience, we can be assured that we will be changed and come to a greater understanding of His unique love for each of us.

In Revelation 4:1, we are provided yet another open invitation to join Christ in the heavenlies. It states, **"After this I looked, and there before me was a door standing open in heaven. And the voice I had first heard speaking to me like a trumpet said "Come up here."** As I read this Scripture, I noted the commanding nature of the direction given in the passage. The Lord is not saying "Come up here when you have time," or "Come up here when you're in the mood," but instead, simply **"Come up here."** In other words, as Christians, we are faced with an unconditional command to spend time in the heavenly realm with Christ. It is not a suggestion or an option. Time spent in the heavens is the greatest form of rest, and we must not miss out on it.

Learning to Say "No"

As we spend time communing with the Lord in the heavenly realm, we will become increasingly familiar with His voice. In addition to spiritual implications, this also has benefits in the natural. For instance, when we are tempted to book our schedules and allow no time for rest, a clear word from the Lord will steer us in the right direction when we have trained ourselves to listen to Him.

Over the past few years, I have come to realize that not every *good* opportunity is a *God* opportunity. The world and the church are both filled with wonderful and noble causes into which we could potentially pour our time and energy. Most church members would agree that it is not unrealistic to receive several calls each week from different facets of the ministry vying for help, time, leadership, or expertise. Learning to rest in the Lord is learning to discern which of these opportunities are truly a part of His vision of ministry for us, and which of them will only wear us out or take time away from the things He has called us to do. When every member of the body of Christ is doing only the work he or she is called to do, ministry will function at its best and believers will be rested and renewed.

> TIME SPENT IN THE HEAVENS IS THE GREATEST FORM OF REST, AND WE MUST NOT MISS OUT ON IT.

Putting the Pieces Together

Ironically, learning to rest in the Lord may actually seem like work at the beginning. It will require new priorities, schedule adjustments, and most of all, a level of faith that spans deeper and wider than we have ever gone before. It is a challenge and a call for every believer, but will become a major key in allowing us to walk in the authority and power the Lord has intended for each of us. Time is short, and change must start now. ∎

TRUE MEASURE of SUCCESS

by Mike Roberts

There are many different kinds of people in the world. They are from different cultures and walks of life, and they have different beliefs and pursuits. If you ask a group of children what they want to be when they are older, you will receive a wide variety of answers. However, in spite of all the various aspirations, goals, and ideas, there is one desire that is true of nearly every person—the desire to be successful.

Success has been defined in a wide variety of ways, and probably every person has their own individual idea of what it means for them personally. Many of these ideas are valid, but for a Christian, success can be defined as "accomplishing the purpose of the Lord for your life." Perhaps one of the most

regrettable moments for a person would be to stand at the end of his life and realize that he had not accomplished what God intended for him to do.

What would that person not give to be able to go back and try again? Would any price be too great to pay for a second chance? Thankfully, most of us are not at the end of our lives, and it is not too late to make a course correction if necessary. We can begin to take steps right now to ensure that we will not fall short of accomplishing what God has called us to do.

Our Primary Calling and Purpose

As Christians, our calling and purpose basically has three parts: 1) to walk with the Lord and know Him intimately, 2) to become like Him, and 3) to fulfill the individual destinies He has placed upon our lives.

Let us examine the first part of this calling. When we are born again, we inherit eternal life. In John 17:3 Jesus said:

"And this is eternal life, that they may know Thee, the only true God, and Jesus Christ whom Thou hast sent."

> It is important to understand that the things Paul counted as loss were things that many people would count as success.

Eternal life does not begin when we die, but it begins as soon as we begin a relationship with the Lord. This relationship is the first part of our calling and purpose. C.S. Lewis once said, "Once a man is united to God, how could he not live forever? Once a man is separated from God, what can he do but wither and die?" Success in this life begins with knowing the Lord; He is the Source of all true life. The apostle Paul understood this. With all he had accomplished, near the end of his life he said:

But whatever things were gain to me, those things I have counted as loss for the sake for Christ.

More than that, I count all things to be loss in view of the surpassing value of *knowing Christ Jesus my Lord*, for whom I have suffered the loss of all things, and count them but rubbish in order that I may gain Christ (Philippians 3:7-8, emphasis mine).

It is important to understand that the things Paul counted as loss were things that many people would count as success. He could have boasted in his own accomplishments, but he chose to disregard them because he understood that success begins with knowing the Lord.

Jesus also talked about this:

"Not everyone who says to Me, 'Lord, Lord,' will enter the kingdom of heaven; but he who does the will of My Father who is in heaven.

"Many will say to Me on that day, 'Lord, Lord, did we not prophesy in Your name, and in Your name cast out demons, and in Your name perform many miracles?'

"And then I will declare to them, '*I never knew you*; DEPART FROM ME, YOU WHO PRACTICE LAWLESSNESS'" (Matthew 7:21-23, emphasis mine).

These people had prophesied, cast out demons, and worked miracles in the name of the Lord, but Jesus said they were workers of lawlessness because what they did was not done on the foundation of knowing the Lord. Knowing Him is the basis of all true success. Whether we are businessmen, carpenters, parents, teachers, pastors, athletes, or whatever our occupation, all true success is founded upon an intimate relationship with the Lord.

Becoming Like the Lord

The second part of our calling and purpose is to become like the Lord. Matthew 5:48 says:

> **"Therefore you are to be perfect, as your heavenly Father is perfect."**

Our natural tendency is to be imperfect and actually rebel against God. However, He has made it possible for us to become like Him, and it starts with knowing Him. II Peter 1:3-4 says:

> **seeing that His divine power has granted to us everything pertaining to life and godliness, through *the true knowledge of Him* who called us by His own glory and excellence.**

> **For by these He has granted to us His precious and magnificent promises, in order that by them you might *become partakers of the divine nature*, having escaped the corruption that is in the world by lust.**

Paul also understood this, as he said in a similar passage:

> **if indeed you have heard Him and have been taught in Him, just as truth is in Jesus,**

> **that, in reference to your former manner of life, you lay aside the old self, which is being corrupted in accordance with the lusts of deceit,**

> **and that you be renewed in the spirit of your mind,**

> **and put on the new self, which *in the likeness of God* has been created in righteousness and holiness of the truth (Ephesians 4:21-24,** emphasis mine).

> **It is through the true knowledge of Him that we access His divine power, which provides us with all that we need for both life and godliness.**

As we grow in our relationship with the Lord, we become transformed into His image and likeness. It is through the true knowledge of Him that we access His divine power, which provides us with all we need for both life and godliness. As we partake of the Lord's nature, our works will also become like His: We will begin to talk, think, and act like the Lord. We will begin to do the works that He did.

The Works of Jesus

When we consider the works of Jesus, many different things come to mind: He raised the dead, healed sick people, restored relationships, forgave the unlovable, and many other remarkable deeds. As John pointed out, if all that Jesus did had been recorded, the world itself would not be able to contain all the books that would have been written (see John 21:25).

We are called to do the very same works Jesus did, and even greater works than His (see John 14:12). If we are to truly fulfill this, it is also important that we understand why Jesus did what He did. In John 5:19 Jesus said:

> ..."Truly, truly, I say to you, the Son can do nothing of Himself, unless it is something He sees the Father doing; for whatever the Father does, these things the Son does in like manner.

Jesus only did the things He saw the Father doing. Rick Joyner has often explained that Jesus never responded to human need, but He was led by the Holy Spirit and only did what He saw His Father do. As we read earlier in Matthew 7, there were people who did many of the same works Jesus did, but they were not done on the basis of seeing the Lord and being led by the Spirit. That is why Jesus referred to their works as works of lawlessness. However, as we see Him and are led by His Spirit, we become like Him and our works will truly become like His.

Our Personal Destiny

As we have seen, our calling and purpose begin with knowing the Lord and becoming like Him. This brings us to the third part of our calling, which is to fulfill our own personal destinies. The Lord told Jeremiah:

> **"Before I formed you in the womb I knew you, and before you were born I consecrated you; I have appointed you a prophet to the nations"** (Jeremiah 1:5).

> ...if all that Jesus did had been recorded, the world itself would not be able to contain all the books that would have been written...

Ephesians 2:10 says,

> **For we are His workmanship, created in Christ Jesus for good works, which God prepared beforehand, that we should walk in them.**

Before we were born and even before God formed us in the womb, He had already prepared good works for us to do. There is a special destiny on each life that is individual and unique. This is very exciting and surely every person desires to fulfill this great calling. But, sadly, many people do not. God has deposited gifts and talents in each person, but many people never fully access them, and they fall short of God's fullness in their lives. Let us examine a few common reasons for this.

Are You Old Enough?

One very common enemy that robs many people of their destiny is the deception that we have to be a certain age to fulfill what God has called us to do. The Lord has a purpose for every person, regardless of his or her age. The Bible is full of dynamic examples of remarkable exploits, and young people did many of them. David, Joseph, Jesus' mother Mary, Daniel, Josiah, Esther, and many others achieved extraordinary things for the Lord at an early age. The same is true today. Paul told Timothy:

> **Let no one look down on your youthfulness, but rather in speech, conduct, love, faith, and purity, show yourself an example of those who believe (I Timothy 4:12).**

As the Lord told Jeremiah, He had a purpose for us before we were even born. If we are waiting until a certain age to begin stepping into it, we will certainly miss out on many things God wants to do today.

Our Sphere of Influence

There has been a mentality, prevalent throughout much of the church which says that a person can never really step into his purpose until he is in full-time, occupational ministry. This misunderstanding has robbed many people from entering into their purpose.

Randall Worley once said, "Many of us have been waiting for God to birth the kingdom out of the church, but God wants to birth the church out of the kingdom." Jesus never preached the gospel of the church, but He preached the gospel of the kingdom, and He wants to manifest the kingdom wherever we are. Regardless of our occupation, God desires to manifest Himself in us and through us to those within our sphere of influence.

If God has called us to be in occupational ministry, then He will bring that about at the appropriate time. However, let us not fall short of His purpose for us in this present season of our lives. Let us go wherever the Lord sends us and view it as an opportunity to be lights in the darkness and reclaim ground that belongs to the Lord.

Quality, Not Quantity

A third common enemy to our purpose and destiny is the idea that we must wait until our circumstances are ideal and allow us to "do more for the Lord." Most Christians have great intentions to one day accomplish something great for God, but many never start because they feel like what they have is not adequate, particularly if they compare themselves with someone else who appears to be able to do more.

> We will never be able to feed everybody who is hungry or help everyone who needs it, but we can reach out to help those who are within our ability to touch.

Legendary basketball coach John Wooden used to tell his players: "Do not let what you cannot do interfere with what you can do." How many times has the enemy robbed us of our potential by telling us the opposite? He would have us focus on what we cannot do so that we do nothing. We may not be able to give ten thousand dollars to the poor right now, but we cannot let that keep us from giving the twenty dollars that we can give. We may not be able to travel and lay hands on the sick and afflicted in Africa and China today, but we can pray for our neighbors in the backyard or our co-workers in the break room. The Lord wants us to start where we are and not wait until we are where we think we should be.

Mother Teresa once said, "If you can't feed one hundred people, feed just one." We will never be able to feed everybody who is hungry or help everyone who needs it, but we can reach out to help those who are within our ability to touch. Wade Taylor once noted: "The important thing is that the will of God is being done in our lives. When we stand before the Lord, He's not going to say 'much done,' He is going to say 'well done.'" At the end of our lives, the Lord is not going to measure our success by what we did, but by what we could have done with the abilities He provided for us.

Conclusion

True success is not measured by our net worth, how early we retire, or how much fame and notoriety we achieve. On the contrary, our natural status and positions are a means to an end—that we fulfill the calling and purpose that God has destined for us.

This calling begins with knowing the Lord and walking with Him in a personal relationship. The second part of our purpose is, as we walk with Him, we become like Him. This enables us to fulfill the third part of our calling—to fulfill the individual destinies He has planned for us.

Let us determine to move forward confident that God **has saved us, and called us with a holy calling, not according to our works, but according to His own purpose and grace which was granted us in Christ Jesus from all eternity"** (II Timothy 1:9). ∎

DOCTRINES OF DEMONS

by Rick Joyner, Robin McMillan, Matt Peterson

The following is taken from an article that was first published in our Prophetic Bulletin just a couple of years ago. Since that time we have become increasingly alarmed as seemingly stable Christians continue to be swept up by these deceptions. It is for this reason that I felt the need to revise and republish this through every means that we have available to us with the hope of sparing as many as possible from these deadly doctrines of demons as the Scriptures call them. (see I Timothy 4:1 NKJV)

—Rick Joyner

In recent years a number of ancient heresies have begun sweeping through the church again, deceiving thousands, even side-tracking whole movements. These are the very same deceptions that tried to seduce the first century church, which much of the New Testament was written to combat. These gain inroads by the most subtle, seemingly innocent ways, but quickly begin to erode the very foundations of Christianity to the point where those who continue in them are actually **"severed from Christ"** (Galatians 5:4) in the very way that the Scriptures warn will happen. We read in I Timothy 4:1-6:

> **Now the Spirit expressly says that in latter times some will depart from the faith, giving heed to deceiving spirits and doctrines of demons,**
>
> **speaking lies in hypocrisy, having their own conscience seared with a hot iron,**

forbidding to marry, and commanding to abstain from foods which God created to be received with thanksgiving by those who believe and know the truth.

For every creature of God is good, and nothing is to be refused if it is received with thanksgiving;

for it is sanctified by the word of God and prayer.

If you instruct the brethren in these things, you will be a good minister of Jesus Christ, nourished in the words of faith and of the good doctrine which you have carefully followed (NKJV).

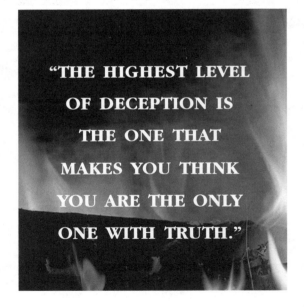

"THE HIGHEST LEVEL OF DECEPTION IS THE ONE THAT MAKES YOU THINK YOU ARE THE ONLY ONE WITH TRUTH."

These doctrines are so blatantly contrary to Scripture that we did not think they had a chance to succeed in the church. However, we were wrong about this, and have been shocked as we have seen some of the seemingly most solid, faithful believers being carried away with these deceptions. Most individuals quickly become isolated, and then they are deceived to the point of even denying the cross and are returning to various forms of legalism for righteousness—even the Law of Moses, just as the previous Scriptures warn that we would see in the last days.

As my prophetic friend, Bob Jones, recently stated in regard to these same doctrines, "The highest level of deception is the one that makes you think you are the only one with truth." That is both a biblical and historical reality. Once a person or a group embraces that delusion, they become nearly unteachable, uncorrectable, and can rarely be recovered. We should be most wary of any person, spirit, or group that tries to make us think that way. Even when Elijah began to think that way, the Lord immediately told him to anoint a successor and took him home before he had completed his commission. It is one of the most dangerous deceptions we could ever embrace and will almost certainly end one's usefulness to the Lord when it is embraced.

Denying the Cross by Turning to the Law

One doctrine that is seeking to make inroads into the church requires Christians to eat in accordance with the Jewish law. It declares that those who do not eat this way are not only in disobedience to God, but have opened themselves up to demons. Some even go so far as to say that those who do not comply with these dietary laws cannot be healed by the Lord and are even in jeopardy of losing their salvation.

In the Scripture quoted above **"commanding to abstain from foods"** is named as a doctrine of demons empowered by deceiving spirits. This does seem to be the entry point of a host of other deceptions that begin to erode the very foundations of the biblical Christian faith. As this verse declares, this form of legalism is a major way that many will **"depart from the faith"** in the last days.

> THESE HERETICAL TEACHERS MUST UNDERMINE THE AUTHORITY OF THE NEW TESTAMENT TO SPREAD THEIR DECEPTION.

The biblical antidote to these heresies is also given, which is, **"If you instruct the brethren in these things, you will be a good minister of Jesus Christ, nourished in the words of faith and of the good doctrine which you have carefully followed"** (I Timothy 4:6).

Because so much of the New Testament was written to counter these very doctrines that were assaulting the first century church, these heretical teachers must undermine the authority of the New

Testament to spread their deception. This is usually done in a most subtle, but systematic way. After seeking to have believers return to the Old Testament as the true basis of faith, they begin to challenge, especially the apostle Paul, as a deviant teacher. Of course, they overlook the fact that all of the apostles and elders of the early church agreed with Paul, which was clearly established in the Council of Jerusalem, and repeatedly affirmed in their own epistles to the church. The conclusion of the Council in Jerusalem was summed up in Acts 15:22-29:

> **Then it seemed good to the apostles and the elders, with the whole church, to choose men from among them to send to Antioch with Paul and Barnabas—Judas called Barsabbas, and Silas, leading men among the brethren,**
>
> **and they sent this letter by them, "The apostles and the brethren who are elders, to the brethren in Antioch and Syria and Cilicia who are from the Gentiles, greetings.**
>
> **"Since we have heard that some of our number to whom we gave no instruction have disturbed you with their words, unsettling your souls,**
>
> **it seemed good to us, having become of one mind, to select men to send to you with our beloved Barnabas and Paul,**
>
> **"men who have risked their lives for the name of our Lord Jesus Christ.**

"Therefore we have sent Judas and Silas, who themselves will also report the same things by word of mouth.

"For it seemed good to the Holy Spirit and to us to lay upon you no greater burden than these essentials:

"that you abstain from things sacrificed to idols and from blood and from things strangled and from fornication; if you keep yourselves free from such things, you will do well. Farewell."

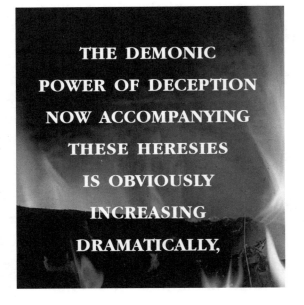

THE DEMONIC POWER OF DECEPTION NOW ACCOMPANYING THESE HERESIES IS OBVIOUSLY INCREASING DRAMATICALLY,

In his letters, Paul addressed this issue of dietary legalism with clear and specific teaching, not only because it would emerge to some degree in every generation, but because, as he stated in I Timothy 4:6, in the last days it would be backed by demonic power and promoted by deceiving spirits. The demonic power of deception now accompanying these heresies is obviously increasing dramatically, subduing many with a spirit of deception that seems nearly impossible to penetrate.

Deception is deceptive and those who fall into it obviously do not know it. Even though the contradictions in these doctrines are often so blatant as to seem ridiculous, they cannot be seen by those who come under their spell. Soon even the most clear, biblical teachings that counter these deceptions have no effect on them as they will often boldly and shockingly twist Scriptures to verify these false doctrines. They shamelessly try to apply every reference to commandments or laws in the New Testament to the Law of Moses, replacing the "new commandments" of love the Lord gave to us, which actually fulfill the Law—the perfect **"law of liberty"(James 1:25)**.

Because these heresies, some of which have their origin in Messianic movements are modern attempts to again bring the church under the yoke of the Law, many are starting to strongly react to all Messianic movements. This is unfortunate as many of the Messianic leaders that we have discussed this with not only recognize these heresies for what they are, but are likewise alarmed by them and are beginning to take strong stands against them. Some readily consider these heresies another form of replacement theology.

Other Messianic groups are still wrestling with these issues, but those who are sincere lovers of truth will come out of this with a strong devotion to the liberty that we have been given in Christ.

That liberty can never be compromised without the most tragic consequences for anyone who trusts in the atonement of the cross. In Galatians 2:11-14, we see in the first century that even Peter, the "apostle to the Jews," along with Barnabas and others were temporarily ensnared with this deception while visiting Antioch.

There can be no compromise with the one essential truth that any doctrine which seeks to displace the cross of Jesus as the only atonement for sin and the only source of righteousness is a heresy of the most dangerous kind. As the Scriptures warn, this can actually sever us from Christ. As we are assured, **"For all the law is fulfilled in one word, even in this: 'You shall love your neighbor as yourself'" (Galatians 5:14).**

Those who are being carried away with this modern form of the ancient heresy usually do exactly as we are told in Romans 10:3-4:

> **For they being ignorant of God's righteousness, and seeking to establish their own righteousness, have not submitted to the righteousness of God.**
>
> **For *Christ is the end of the law for righteousness* to everyone who believes (NKJV).**

The Law itself declares that if we are guilty of not keeping a single commandment, we are guilty of breaking the whole Law. If we are going to keep the whole Law, we will have to return to making the sacrifices required by the Law, not to mention the stoning of not only adulterers (Leviticus 20:10),

homosexuals (Leviticus 20:13), or those who seek to entice us away from the Lord (Deuteronomy 13:6-11), but even stubborn, rebellious children (Deuteronomy 21:18-21), as well as anyone who breaks the Sabbath (Numbers 15:32-36).

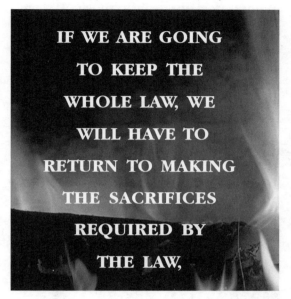

IF WE ARE GOING TO KEEP THE WHOLE LAW, WE WILL HAVE TO RETURN TO MAKING THE SACRIFICES REQUIRED BY THE LAW,

Because of this, the modern Judaizers blatantly pick and choose the parts of the Law that they think should be kept today and disregard the rest. This, among other things, makes for many contradictions in their teachings that are amazingly overlooked by their followers. Again, deception is deceptive. We see how Paul tried to warn those who were foolishly falling to this in his own time:

> **For Moses writes about the righteousness which is of the law, "The man who does those things shall live by them" (Romans 10:5).**
>
> **And I testify again to every man who becomes circumcised that he is a debtor to keep the whole law (Galatians 5:3 NKJV).**

If we adhered to the Law of Moses today, how many of us would have had to kill our own children? Indeed, if our parents had kept the Law regarding stoning rebellious children, how many of us would be here now? This, of course, might especially apply to those of us who grew up in the 60s! How many of us who now serve the Lord in truth would have never made it through the adultery that many of us lived in before Christ? How many homosexuals would have had no chance for deliverance and salvation? And how could anyone escape the kind of judgment the Law brings when the simple act of picking up sticks on the Sabbath resulted in death by stoning?

GOD'S ONLY REMEDY FOR SIN IS THE CROSS, AND THE MERCY OF GOD THAT TRIUMPHS OVER JUDGMENT IS ONLY FOUND THERE.

The Law rightly established the standards of God's righteousness, and the fact that the consequence of sin is death. However, it was a tutor to lead us to Christ by revealing the standards of God's righteousness and exposing sin, compelling us to fall at the foot of the cross for our salvation and find our righteousness in Christ. God's only remedy for sin is the cross, and the mercy of God that triumphs over judgment is only found there.

Since the Law simply could not be "digested" by fallen man, those who returned to the Law for righteousness in the first century were referred to as "dogs" (see II Peter 2:22). This is because dogs will return to and try to eat their own vomit. Paul wrote in Philippians 3:2-9:

> **Beware of the dogs, beware of the evil workers, beware of the false circumcision;**
>
> **for we are the true circumcision, who worship in the Spirit of God and glory in Christ Jesus and put no confidence in the flesh,**
>
> **although I myself might have confidence even in the flesh. If anyone else has a mind to put confidence in the flesh, I far more:**
>
> **circumcised the eighth day, of the nation of Israel, of the tribe of Benjamin, a Hebrew of Hebrews; as to the Law, a Pharisee;**
>
> **as to zeal, a persecutor of the church; as to the righteousness which is in the Law, found blameless.**
>
> **But whatever things were gain to me, those things I have counted as loss for the sake of Christ.**
>
> **More than that, I count all things to be loss in view of the surpassing value of knowing**

Christ Jesus my Lord, for whom I have suffered the loss of all things, and count them but rubbish in order that I may gain Christ,

and may be found in Him, not having a righteousness of my own derived from the Law, but that which is through faith in Christ, the righteousness which comes from God on the basis of faith.

Concerning His city, in Revelation 22:15 the Lord says: **"Outside are the dogs and the sorcerers and the immoral persons and the murderers and the idolaters, and everyone who loves and practices lying."** This is not a very good group to be counted with, but such is the lot of those who try to return to the Law to establish their own righteousness.

God's Method of Revealing Salvation to the Gentiles

What would be harder for God, to redeem a food group or an entire people group? In revealing to the apostle Peter that His salvation was for every people group, He revealed to him that he could now eat things that were formerly condemned by the Law. God went to great extremes to prove to Peter that He could cleanse anything and anyone as we read in Acts 10:9-20. This led Peter to open the door of faith to the Gentiles by going to the house of Cornelius, a Roman centurion. As he was preaching the gospel, he and his party of circumcised Jews were amazed as they witnessed the outpouring of the Holy Spirit upon the Gentiles gathered there.

Even in light of these remarkable events, the Jewish believers in Jerusalem contended with Peter about the salvation of the Gentiles, **"...saying, 'You went in to uncircumcised men and ate with them"(Acts 11:3).** Nevertheless it was true. God had cleansed a people group by convincing Peter he could also cleanse a food group which he had seen in his vision.

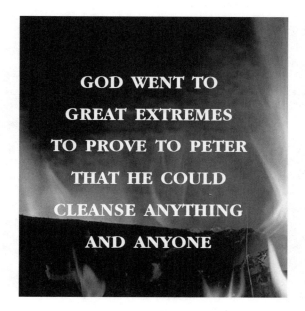

GOD WENT TO GREAT EXTREMES TO PROVE TO PETER THAT HE COULD CLEANSE ANYTHING AND ANYONE

It is noteworthy that this took place in Joppa, the same city where Jonah rejected God's call to the Ninevites. Thankfully, Simon *Bar Jonah (or "Son of Jonah")* was willing to receive new revelation from God which went against centuries of teaching that had dominated the Jewish mindset when God wrought a substantive change in many dimensions by the death, burial, and resurrection of Christ Jesus.

Yet this issue continued to plague the young church. For this reason Paul wrote to the Corinthian church:

Eat whatever is sold in the meat market, asking no questions for conscience's sake;

for the earth is the LORD'S, and all its fullness" (I Corinthians 10:25-26).

To the church at Rome he wrote:

Receive one who is weak in the faith, but not to disputes over doubtful things.

For one believes he may eat all things, but he who is weak eats only vegetables.

Let not him who eats despise him who does not eat, and let not him who does not eat judge him who eats; for God has received him.

Who are you to judge another's servant? To his own master he stands or falls. Indeed, he will be made to stand, for God is able to make him stand.

One person esteems one day above another; another esteems every day alike. Let each be fully convinced in his own mind.

He who observes the day, observes it to the Lord; and he who does not observe the day, to the Lord he does not observe it. He who eats, eats to the Lord, for he gives God thanks; and he who does not eat, to the Lord he does not eat, and gives God thanks.

For none of us lives to himself, and no one dies to himself.

For if we live, we live to the Lord; and if we die, we die to the Lord. Therefore, whether we live or die, we are the Lord's (Romans 14:1-8 NKJV).

Paul was convinced by the Lord Jesus Himself that nothing is unclean of itself.

I know and am convinced by the Lord Jesus that there is nothing unclean of itself; but to him who considers anything to be unclean, to him it is unclean (Romans 14:14 NKJV).

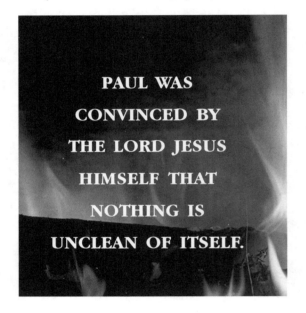

PAUL WAS CONVINCED BY THE LORD JESUS HIMSELF THAT NOTHING IS UNCLEAN OF ITSELF.

When Paul used the Greek word "koinos" for unclean or common, it was the word both Peter and the Lord used in Acts 11:8-9. "But I said, 'Not so, Lord! For nothing *common* or unclean has at any time entered my mouth.' "But the voice answered me again from heaven, 'What God has cleansed you must not call *common*'" (NKJV). If God could not cleanse all food, how could He cleanse all of mankind?

To the Colossians Paul wrote:

> So let no one judge you in food or in drink, or regarding a festival or a new moon or sabbaths,
>
> which are a shadow of things to come, but the substance is of Christ.
>
> Let no one cheat you of your reward, taking delight in false humility and worship of angels, intruding into those things which he has not seen, vainly puffed up by his fleshly mind,
>
> and not holding fast to the Head, from whom all the body, nourished and knit together by joints and ligaments, grows with the increase that is from God.
>
> Therefore, if you died with Christ from the basic principles of the world, why, as though living in the world, do you subject yourselves to regulations—
>
> "Do not touch, do not taste, do not handle,"
>
> which all concern things which perish with the using—according to the commandments and doctrines of men?
>
> These things indeed have an appearance of wisdom in self-imposed religion, false humility, and neglect of the body, but are of no value against the indulgence of the flesh (Colossians 2:16-23 NKJV).

Jesus Himself addressed this same issue:

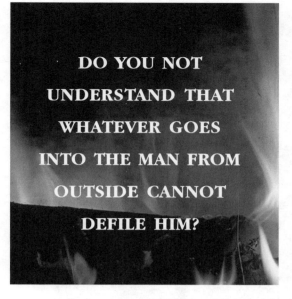

DO YOU NOT UNDERSTAND THAT WHATEVER GOES INTO THE MAN FROM OUTSIDE CANNOT DEFILE HIM?

> After He called the multitude to Him again, He began saying to them, "Listen to Me, all of you, and understand:
>
> there is nothing outside the man which going into him can defile him; but the things which proceed out of the man are what defile the man.
>
> ["If any man has ears to hear, let him hear."]
>
> And when leaving the multitude, He had entered the house, His disciples questioned Him about the parable.
>
> And He said to them, "Are you so lacking in understanding also? Do you not understand that whatever goes into the man from outside cannot defile him;
>
> because it does not go into his heart, but into his stomach, and is eliminated?" (Thus He declared all foods clean.)

And He was saying, "That which proceeds out of the man, that is what defiles the man.

"For from within, out of the heart of men, proceed the evil thoughts, fornications, thefts, murders, adulteries,

deeds of coveting and wickedness, as well as deceit, sensuality, envy, slander, pride and foolishness.

"All these evil things proceed from within and defile the man" (Mark 7:14-23).

> EACH INDIVIDUAL IS FREE TO ADOPT HIS OR HER OWN CODE OF DIET AND SHOULD NOT APPLY PRESSURE UPON ONE ANOTHER IN THESE AREAS.

Jesus taught that it is what is in a man's heart, not what enters into his mouth that defiles him. That is why heart faith is required to purify a man, heart faith is the work that Jesus Christ has done on our behalf. It is His blood that has cleansed us, not our adherence to any body of laws.

Eating for Health

While it is true that eating habits have a significant affect upon one's health, it is also clear from the sum of both Jesus' and Paul's biblical teachings that they did not teach that eating according to the Levitical code was a New Covenant commandment from God. They taught the very opposite.

To follow one's conscience in areas not specifically addressed in Scripture is a fundamental aspect of New Testament freedom for which the Lord died. It is also clear that the church is *not* to establish such dietary rules as either commands or requirements for its membership. Each individual is free to adopt his or her own code of diet and should not apply pressure upon one another in these areas. It was for freedom that Christ set us free. Let us therefore have the courage and resolve to maintain the following apostolic charge:

Stand fast therefore in the liberty by which Christ has made us free, and do not be entangled again with a yoke of bondage.

Indeed I, Paul, say to you that if you become circumcised, Christ will profit you nothing.

And I testify again to every man who becomes circumcised that he is a debtor to keep the whole law.

You have become estranged from Christ, you who attempt to be justified by law; you have fallen from grace.

For we through the Spirit eagerly wait for the hope of righteousness by faith.

For in Christ Jesus neither circumcision nor un-circumcision avails anything, but faith working through love (Galatians 5:1-6 NKJV).

The Judaizers made circumcision a main issue in the first century, but the same principles hold true for any aspect of the Law that is thrust upon believers as a means of establishing their standing before God in place of the cross.

The main inroads of the modern version seem to be re-establishing the dietary rules of the Law of Moses. This is an inroad that seems to inevitably lead to other heresies. However, there are some who advocate eating according to the Law simply for health reasons, and these should not be confused with those who compel believers to keep the dietary laws as a form of obedience to God.

A Devastating New Form of Slavery for African-Americans

One of the offshoots of these aberrant teachings is the attempt to Judaize African Americans and Native Americans by making them think that they are members of the lost tribes of Israel. Compelling believers to return to the Law was referred to by the New Testament apostles as bringing them again under the yoke of slavery (see Galatians 5:1), and this is precisely what this new form of the ancient heresy is attempting to do. When it especially targets African-Americans who have only in recent history been freed from physical slavery, this spiritual slavery is even more than ironic—it is the kind of tragic cruelty of which only the devil is capable.

Several Messianic and other leaders have observed that those who fall to this kind of deception are in most cases lacking a strong personal identity and are therefore easily drawn to seek an identity as one of "God's chosen people." This can only happen to those who fail to understand that the ultimate identity is to be found in Christ as a "new creation."

COMPELLING BELIEVERS TO RETURN TO THE LAW WAS REFERRED TO BY THE NEW TESTAMENT APOSTLES AS BRINGING THEM AGAIN UNDER THE YOKE OF SLAVERY...

We are told in II Corinthians 5:16-17:

Therefore from now on we recognize no man according to the flesh; even though we have known Christ according to the flesh, yet now we know Him thus no longer.

Therefore if any man is in Christ, he is a new creature; the old things passed away; behold, new things have come.

As stated, such deceptions are only possible because of a basic lack of understanding of the new creation that we are called to be. However, many

Christians lack these basic foundational teachings. This deception is not only making inroads among African-American churches, but throughout the church. One of the most popular forms of this teaching is called "British Israelism." It tries to establish the British as the lost tribes of Israel (the northern ten tribes that were scattered and lost to history).

> ONLY THOSE LACKING A VERY BASIC UNDERSTANDING OF WHO THEY ARE IN CHRIST WOULD BE SO CONCERNED ABOUT WHO THEY ARE IN THE FLESH.

There has also been a book published that seeks to establish the Japanese as the lost tribes of Israel. It seems apparent that sooner or later they will try to convince everyone that they are the lost tribes of Israel. Actually, the arguments are quite compelling, and there probably is some truth to it. In fact, it is likely that all races now have some ancestors from these lost tribes.

So what? Those who are in Christ, who are of the new creation, are first generation descendents of God! Only those lacking a very basic understanding of who they are in Christ would be so concerned about who they are in the flesh. Only those who are weak in their identity in Christ will be drawn to being made to feel special or to be included in a special group in such a way as this. The fact is that many are weak in their identity in Christ, and they are easy prey for such deceivers.

Attacking the Only Name by Which We Are Saved

Another aberrant offshoot of this doctrine seeks to establish that the name "Jesus" is a pagan name, and we should therefore only use the name Yeshua, which is the "proper Hebrew name." They also reject other names for the Father but Yahweh, which in itself is a human derivative for what is supposed to be "the un-pronounceable name of God." If it is "un-pronounceable," why try to pronounce it at all?" Even so, what kind of father would demand his children to call him by his full, proper name before answering them? This may seem too outrageous for anyone to buy into, but many have.

God is not as petty as these foolishly suppose. The Lord still heals in "the name of Jesus." Even the demons recognize that name and obey it. The Lord knows when you call upon Him regardless of which language you use. Witchcraft is based on formulas and incantations, and we must grow up and start rejecting such ridiculous doctrines that these foolish and deceived people are trying to impose upon believers. If you accept them, you will drift from being a believer and become one who tries to establish your own righteousness by being a performer, severed from Christ Who is our righteousness.

We should also keep in mind that there are many solid believers who prefer to use the name Yeshua for various reasons, which should in no way reflect on their spiritual character. However, we must understand that demons hate the name of Jesus because they know its power, and we should be wary of any person who seeks to undermine His name in any form. They are obviously being demonically influenced at best.

The Antidote

The antidote to these poisons that some are trying to feed the church is found in the first verses we quoted in this message from I Timothy 4:1-6. We must instruct God's people in these things and fortify the basic doctrines of the faith that many are drifting from.

In this article, we have only superficially dealt with these heresies and have refrained from naming specific teachers of these doctrines or their books. However, we are not averse to naming them in order to protect the church, as this has an obvious precedent in the New Testament. If they continue to make inroads in the church, we will deal with them as becomes necessary, probably addressing them in future editions of *The Morning Star Journal*. We must confront such heresies or we will never be true shepherds or watchmen. If they are making inroads into your church or movement, they must likewise be confronted if you are going to be a true shepherd or watchman.

Everything we need to confront such aberrant teachings is in the New Testament, which was written primarily to confront the roots of probably every false doctrine that continues to try to gain access to the church. The book of Galatians was specifically written to address the heresy we have addressed here. I strongly recommend that every believer read the entire New Testament every year. This can be done in just over six months by reading a single chapter a day.

WE MUST REJECT ANYTHING WHICH TRIES TO ECLIPSE HIM AS THE ONE WHO ALONE IS THE WAY, THE TRUTH, AND OUR LIFE.

We should also not let this kind of aberrant teaching cause us to overreact and keep us from reading the Old Testament. Every place in the New Testament which refers to **"the Scriptures"** is in reference to the Old Testament. However, we must do so from a strong foundation of understanding the New Covenant, seeing how the Old Testament points to and prepares us for the New Covenant in Christ. Basically it is "all about Jesus." We must reject anything which tries to eclipse Him as the One Who alone is the Way, the Truth, and our Life. ∎

MARKETPLACE Encounter

by Tom Archer

As an Federal Aviation Administration (FAA) test pilot, I often travel to different manufacturers to test fly their new aircraft. On one such occasion, my wife, Jackie, and I traveled to a small, economically challenged town. The aircraft manufacturer that we were to visit, employed about fifteen people. The company began in the owner's garage twenty-three years earlier and had grown slowly. Although they had moved to a new facility at the local airport, growth had stagnated as they had been building an average of two airplanes per month for some time. The sale of those airplanes provided the revenue necessary to sustain the company through the next month. At the time of our visit, the company had just begun the arduous process of obtaining FAA certification of a new airplane, and the success of that airplane was to be essential to the survival of the company.

While I was out flying with the owner of the company, Jackie waited in a conference room in the hanger. While there, she prayed for the company and was given some prophetic revelation while observing the bright sunlight coming through the window. The message was this: "You're going to go through a difficult time, but if you keep everything in the light, the Lord will bring you through." She wrote the word down and included Proverbs 3:5-6; "**Trust in the LORD with all your heart, and do not lean on your own understanding. In all your ways acknowledge Him, and He will make your paths straight.**" She delivered the word to the owner after our flight, and we returned home.

During the next year, I heard several reports about how forthcoming the owner was being throughout the certification process, and how graciously he was dealing with the government in the midst of a process that had the potential for being quite frustrating. It made the government employees that much more willing to help him. He told me on one occasion that he had taken to heart the word that Jackie had given him and that things seemed to be as difficult as she had said they would be.

About eighteen months after our visit to that airplane manufacturer, the company received FAA approval of their airplane. Their success was featured in a couple of local newspapers. They are poised to expand their facility, hire one hundred employees, and are projecting sales of thirty airplanes per month by the end of the year. The obedience of one businessman to a prophetic word has resulted in great God-given success for his company, for his community, and for many others. ■

I can see, and that
is why I can be happy,
in what you call the dark,
but which to me is golden.
I can see a God-made world,
not a manmade world.

—Helen Keller

➤➤➤ Mustard Seeds of Wisdom ◀◀◀

The Season of "NEXT TIME!"

by Deborah Joyner Johnson

We are in a wonderful season of new opportunities. Where we have previously failed, we are now being given a second chance to succeed. I was listening to an old song recently and the words rang in my ears after I heard it: "Next time…I'll know better what to do." When I heard those words, I realized the Lord was saying even though we may have failed at something in the past, He is going to give us another chance to do it right "next time."

If we can learn from those difficult experiences of failure in the past, then victory will surely come. Michael Jordan, NBA champion, once made this statement:

I have missed more than 9,000 shots in my career. I have lost almost 300 games. On 26 occasions I have been entrusted to take the game winning shot and I missed. I have failed over and over and over again in my life. And that's precisely why I succeed.

Why did Michael Jordan succeed? He did not stay down when he made mistakes—he learned from them! He practiced more and perfected his shots until he became one of the best basketball players *ever*. When we fail at something, it is not the end, but can actually be the best beginning of all. Those who have accomplished great things in life have known many failures. It is the failures that have actually propelled them to rise up and try harder. If we have learned from our mistakes, then we are in a place to have greater successes in the same areas. The sweetest victories come from rising up and out of failure.

The key to rising up is to have the perseverance to try again. *Webster's Dictionary* describes perseverance like this: "to continue in some effort, course of action, etc. in spite of difficulty, opposition, etc.; be steadfast in purpose; persist." This is precisely what Michael Jordan and multitudes of others have done in the face of defeat, which in turn caused them to become so successful. The lessons from failures will cause us to achieve the greatest victories in our lives if we will persist in learning all that we can from them.

Letting go of the past will allow us to step out of the cold and into the warmth of a new season.

For too long many have stayed down, believing because of their pasts there was no hope for the future. Do not believe it! The past is just that—the past. History repeats itself, both good and bad, so when we are given this "next time" we must take it for the opportunity that it is, and determine to make the outcome positive.

Thomas Edison once responded to a reporter with the following quote after he had failed two thousand times before he successfully invented the light bulb. "I never failed once. It just happened to be a 2000-step process." He saw his experiments with the light bulb as lessons, not failures. He chose to see them as an opportunity for success, rather than the failure that they so seemingly portrayed. He became one of the greatest inventors ever with 1,093 inventions, averaging a patent every two weeks of his working career. As his life portrayed, he knew how to stay focused and persevere until there was success.

Season of Hope

The following Scriptures are for us to remember as we face our "next times."

For behold, the winter is past, the rain is over and gone.

The flowers have already appeared in the land...(Song of Solomon 2:11-12).

"For behold, the winter is past." During winter most activities tend to be inside, simply because it is warmer. But the Lord is saying now **"the winter is past!"** It is time to leave the cold (past failures) and embrace the new. Letting go of the past will allow us to step out of the cold and into the warmth of a new season. Failures can come in many ways— our purpose in life, in relationships, sins, and so on. It is time to rise up and receive forgiveness from the past. Likewise, we must also forgive those who have wronged us, just as the Lord has in His grace forgiven us. As we become free of the past, we will then be in the place to embrace the new things that the Lord will begin to bring forth in our lives.

Perhaps in the past you have never been able to walk forward into your calling. Do not give up! This season holds new hope—a chance for a "next time!" C.S. Lewis once said: "You are never too old to set another goal or to dream a new dream." God is giving you a second chance to fulfill all that you have been called to do. Now is the time to seize the opportunity!

"The rain is over and gone." Rain is necessary for growth and nourishment, for without it a plant would surely die. Rain softens the hard earth and prepares the soil to receive nourishing water. Then, when the plant receives the necessary warmth from the sun, it will grow to new heights. The same is true for us.

We will go through seasons of rain for nourishment, but before that time the Lord has to break up the fallow ground around our hearts to prepare us for the new seeds and growth. We will receive the most from the Lord as we embrace these hard times, looking with hope toward a time of growth. Then the rain will come, nourishing all that the Lord has taught us. When the rain stops, and the "Son" begins to shine upon us, we will begin to grow in many areas of our lives. And in this growing, we will be changed into a new person. From this place of new growth, we will know better what to do when the opportunity arises for a "next time."

"Flowers have already appeared in the land." Summer is the season for flowers to shine in their beauty. They have been lying dormant all winter, but in this season they will bloom into their purpose. As the flowers grow, beauty will be displayed for all to see. Likewise, the same is happening with us. When the "next time" comes, beauty in this season will be seen—not the death of winter, but the warmth and new life of summer. It is time to make right that which has been wrong in the past. This "next time" will be a blessed opportunity to bring forth fruit in what may have seemingly died before.

From this place of new growth, we will know better what to do when the opportunity arises for a "next time."

This season of second chances is a gift from the Lord. We must arise and shine as Isaiah 60:1 states: **"Arise, shine; for your light has come, and the glory of the LORD has risen upon you."** Leave the past behind and embrace the new. Seize this opportunity and fulfill your destiny. His grace is sufficient for this, and so much more. ∎

The Hexagonal Star Over Europe— A VISION

All Scriptures are New International Version unless otherwise indicated.

by Lilo Keller

The following vision was given to me by the Lord on Yom Kippur as a charge to the church. What I saw disturbed me very much. I saw a map of Europe before me, and the continent was covered by a thick dark cloud. It was shaped like a hexagonal star—its tips reaching Portugal, Ireland, Norway, Russia, the Ukraine, Sicily, and Israel. The center of the star was above the German-speaking part of Europe.

There was a beast hidden within the cloud that reached down to earth with his arms clasping to the ground. The beast was only able to hang on where people voluntarily or involuntarily gave him the right to do so. The cloud protected him so he could not be recognized, but with his arms he controlled people, geographic locations, as well as the air space.

Then I saw lights coming on in some places that continued to become brighter. They were red and yellow. The closer I got, the more it became evident to me that they were blazing flames surrounding those who had gathered to worship God. Those places were radiating with the fear of God, with holiness, beauty, and power.

I saw the heat, the light, and the power in some of these places become so strong that the arms of the beast, which looked like tentacles of an octopus, lost their grip on them. They burned up, let go, and withdrew or they simply fell off. Wherever this happened, holes appeared in the canopy of clouds, becoming channels through which the light of heaven and the presence of God could penetrate. Angels ascended and descended serving men.

Embattled Europe

Five years ago, John Mulinde came to the German-speaking nations from Uganda because God had given him a vision of a map of Europe being covered by a thick, dark blanket of clouds until a blinding light pierced through the clouds, causing the beams to soon spread across the entire earth. Then, he heard the passage from Isaiah 60:1-5:

Arise, shine, for your light has come, and the glory of the LORD rises upon you.

See, darkness covers the earth and thick darkness is over the peoples, but the LORD rises upon you and his glory appears over you.

Nations will come to your light, and kings to the brightness of your dawn.

Lift up your eyes and look about you: All assemble and come to you; your sons come from afar, and your daughters are carried on the arm.

Then you will look and be radiant, your heart will throb and swell with joy; the wealth on the seas will be brought to you, to you the riches of the nations will come.

When John Mulinde asked God for the meaning of the vision, God told him: "The darkness you've seen is the power of evil rising up in Europe. It is the power of intense darkness all across the continent. Wherever it can take hold of people it will turn their hearts away from Me. It will cause people to hate Me and to love evil. They will hate everything that is good and holy and everything that is according to My Law. Instead, they will strive for what is evil and worthless. However, I will stretch out My arm to bring revival. There will be enough grace to enable people to make a decision either for Me or against Me. However, this requires for My people to be fully devoted to Me and to seek My face." (Quoted from John Mulinde: *Light or Darkness Over Europe,* Verlag Gottfried Bernard.)

There will be enough grace to enable people to make a decision either for Me or against me.

Five years have passed since then, and we can see how much of what was prophesied by John Mulinde is actually coming to pass. On the one hand, darkness, lawlessness, and the demise of good and order in our country is obvious. Just think about the legislation regarding homosexual civil unions, abortion, or stem cell research, the disappearance of Christian religious instruction in public schools, or the rise of Islam in the western hemisphere. On the other hand, we see the light and the power of the Holy Spirit breaking through in several different places. Growing numbers of New Agers feel drawn to Jesus in search of life. Signs and wonders are on the rise. Prayer movements are forming. Christian youth are rising with a desire to build the kingdom of God together with their spiritual fathers and mothers. New kinds of churches are being established. The gospel is being proclaimed once again in the streets through preaching and music.

Evil is growing and gaining strength while at the same time the kingdom of God is advancing, and the bride of Christ is gaining strength as well. The divide between both movements is widening, and the contrast between light and darkness is becoming ever more striking.

The Hexagonal Canopy of Clouds and the Beast

When I saw the hexagonal star over the map of Europe, I felt immediately reminded of the Star of David, the symbol of the Jews. The many prayer marches, reconciliation events, and repentance services regarding the persecution of the Jews during World War II may lead

us to believe the issue has been settled. God seems to think otherwise.

Yes, God is true to His Word, and whenever we confess our iniquities, He is faithful and just and will forgive us (see I John 1:9). However, I believe God is trying to make us aware of the fact that the "beast" of racism, especially of anti-Semitism and of fascism is hiding within the clouds of an enlightened, humanistic, anti-Christian mindset.

The gospel is being proclaimed once again in the streets through preaching and music.

The tentacles of the beast find a place to attach themselves wherever people give room to this spirit whether consciously or unconsciously—on the one hand by nurturing the idea that the Jews are to blame for everything, and on the other hand by teaching a replacement theology which is still prevalent in many churches. Replacement theology believes that the church has taken the place of the Jewish people, leaving the Jews void of their calling as the chosen people and the apple of God's eye.

One direct consequence of this idea is our attitude toward Israel, frequently portrayed in the way the media reports about the situation in the Middle East which is often biased, overly critical, and many times untrue. Yet, God has committed Himself to Israel in His Word. He has made it clear that those who curse Israel shall not stand (see Genesis 12:3). This does not imply that everything the current Israeli government does is right. However, it does reveal God's purposes for the nation of Israel.

> ...whenever a people humble themselves and repent, the Lord will hear from heaven and extend His hand to bring help and restoration.

Another foothold for the power of the beast is a history of shed innocent blood that causes certain geographic locations to be permanently defiled (see Psalm 106:37-38, Deuteronomy 19:10). Yet, it remains true that whenever a people humble themselves and repent, the Lord will hear from heaven and extend His hand to bring help and restoration.

The Power of Worship

This vision gives us an idea how the strength and influence of this powerful spirit can be broken: Wherever the people of God gather to worship, God will begin to act. In Zechariah 2:5 we read, **"And I myself will be a wall of fire around it,"** declares the LORD, **"and I will be its glory within."** That is what I saw in my vision: holiness, the fear of the Lord, transparence, beauty, and power were amidst the multitudes of worshipers.

The red color of the fire may indicate that these are people who overcome and who are serving the crucified and risen Lord fearlessly, paying no heed to what others may think. They have made the sacrifice of Jesus on the cross the center of their lives and have become witnesses of His resurrection power (see Revelation 12:11). The gold or yellow color may imply that they are on a path of character transformation and sanctification motivated by their fear of the Lord. They buy gold purified by fire (see Revelation 3:18) and they no longer live for themselves, but have put the kingdom of God above all other concerns. Therefore, they have incredible power. They do the **"greater works"** (see John 14:12 NAS) Jesus talked about. No venomous tentacle, no malice, no impurity, no lies, no compromise, no spirit of control can stand in their presence.

I am convinced that we will only begin to discover the overwhelming power of the body of Christ when we come together before our Lord full of bridal love giving Him all power, praise, dominion, and worship.

Open Windows of Heaven

When Jacob awoke from his dream in which he had seen the stairway to heaven with angels ascending and descending, he was afraid and said, **"How awesome is this place! This is none other than the house of God; this is the gate of heaven." Early the next morning Jacob took the stone he had placed under his head and set it up as a pillar and poured oil on top of it. He called that place Bethel"** (which means house of God) **Genesis 28:17-19).**

I believe that corporate worship is God's strategy to create hubs of His power and of His revelation. There will come a time when these gatherings of the saints will be the true legislative centers of cities, regions, and nations as heaven will be open in these places.

Just like Jacob poured oil over the pillar of stones, we are not only to build gathering places of worship, but as the bridal church, we need to keep the fires of worship burning through the power of the Holy Spirit. If we do, they will increase and become so strong that every power of darkness will be pushed back, and the help and protection of the angels, the messengers of God, will be with us.

Let us take courageous steps, like Isaiah encourages us, for God is able to do what He promised. **"Pass through, pass through the gates** (of praise and worship)! **Prepare the way…Remove the stones. Raise a banner for the nations"** (**Isaiah 62:10).** Let us go up to the mountain of worship until the presence of God spreads like wildfire and we will be called a **"holy people,"** and **"the redeemed of the Lord"** (see Isaiah 62:12). ∎

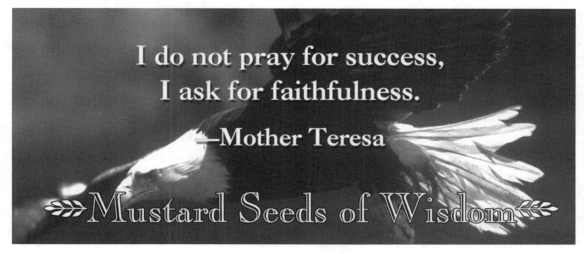

I do not pray for success,
I ask for faithfulness.

—Mother Teresa

≫Mustard Seeds of Wisdom≪

LIGHTHOUSE

by Eric Swisher

The need to explore is strong within us, yet we yearn for home. Lighthouses stand, physically and symbolically, at the places where both are equally possible, and the call is equally strong. They speak to us of going out and coming in, of voyages begun and voyages ended and voyages yet to come. Lighthouses. — *Michael Vogel*

The lighthouse stands at the edge of the familiar and the start of the unknown, and simultaneously represents the comforts of home and the romance of adventure. As such, lighthouses have prophetic significance for 24-hour worship and prayer ministries. These ministries stand at the edge of worship and intercession familiar and comfortable to the church, and at the start of voyages that can be mysterious and even dangerous.

Due to this prophetic connection where the natural can speak of the spiritual, the study of the design and use of lighthouses reveals spiritual parallels for those considering starting or already participating in 24-hour worship and prayer ministries.

History

Most lighthouses do not make it. Their very nature requires they be built in harsh environments, and if constructed wrong, they will not survive. The history of lighthouse design, construction, and maintenance is the continual application of lessons learned from previous mistakes. Presumption in starting or participating in a 24-hour ministry can lead to a frustrating waste of time and resources, and even disaster.

Some lighthouses are counterfeits. "Wreckers" were so named because they placed lights at locations that were certain to result in wrecked vessels and rich cargo. Since God has established the principles for 24-hour worship and prayer in His Word, they should be studied and applied with wisdom, not only for constructing and maintaining an effective ministry, but also for discerning counterfeits.

Foundation

History has shown that it is critical for lighthouses to be constructed with a sound foundation that takes into account the demands of the surrounding environment. The very conditions that require a lighthouse are the very conditions that usually hinder it. Their function dictates that they should be established where the forces of nature will be hell-bent on destroying them. The builder, therefore, cannot over-emphasize the importance of a solid foundation.

Storms

The most powerful function of 24-hour worship is the selah. The basic element of a selah is conflict and resolve. Through the prompting and burdening of the Holy Spirit, in accordance with the Word, the worshipers intercede until God shows up and resolves the conflict. There are many types of selahs, depending on the conflict. In Scripture, one of the most often selahs used is the "storm" selah. Learning

how to deal with storms is a major theme for those called to 24-hour worship.

Some estimates of the energy released by a single storm are on the order of several hundred hydrogen bombs. In a single day, a mature hurricane can expend enough energy to provide the United States with all the power it needs for an entire week. A hurricane can generate waves in the open ocean of 100 feet or higher. A tsunami wave can reach a speed of more than 805 miles an hour. This is why the design and construction of a sure foundation cannot be over-emphasized. Lack of discernment can cause well-meaning worshipers to construct 24-hour ministries without the foundation and equipping necessary to withstand the forces that will come their way.

Many lighthouses have structures made of interlocking, dovetailed granite blocks that hold each other in place. As explained in I Peter 2:5, priests are living stones, being built together as a spiritual house to offer up spiritual sacrifices acceptable to God. The relationships among the core group of 24-hour ministries must be solid, mature, and strongly linked.

If the lighthouse site was dangerous, the dovetailed structures were fitted and assembled on shore, and then moved piecemeal to the construction site for easier and quicker assembly. In areas of high demonic activity, God prepares the worshipers seemingly separate and independent from each other. When it is time, He sovereignly assembles the pieces together in a safe area and then quickly moves them to the lighthouse site giving the workers time to finish the construction before the enemy can attack while it is weak.

The contours of the lighthouse structure are usually designed as a cone or cylinder to minimize potential wind and wave damage. In areas where there is a possibility of extreme weather (such as hurricanes), successful lighthouse structures are built without walls. To be effective, the wise worshiper allows God to deliver them from aspects of their lives that could be vulnerable to enemy attack during selahs.

Erosion and Pollution

Another threat to the lighthouse foundation and structure is erosion and pollution. These slow, insidious, ongoing threats have caused many great lighthouses to be relocated or abandoned. Over time, seemingly harmless sins or attitudes, if unchecked, will seriously erode the effectiveness of 24-hour worship and prayer ministries. That which is not much of a threat to church or evangelistic ministries can be a serious problem for those ministering to the Lord.

Character

Ministries in 24-hour worship/prayer are not higher or more spiritual than any other calling, just different. Lighthouse keepers endure relentless labor in hazardous environments, occasioned by times of drama and danger. Workers can also experience long stretches of boredom and loneliness. The 24-hour worshiper/watchman must, of course, be committed to intimacy for ministering to the Lord, but other important character traits include faithfulness, diligence, dependability, courage, patience, and longsuffering.

The keeper's personal quarters were located adjacent to the lighthouse. Though not mandatory, a 24-hour ministry will be more effective if those who lead it actually live next to the building where the worship takes place. The 24-hour ministry by its very nature tends to be an integral part of the "lighthouse keeper's" home.

Variety

No two lighthouses are the same. The design of each lighthouse varies according to its location, function, and resources. Each site poses unique challenges. A common mistake of 24-hour ministries is to copy other 24-hour ministries, especially those that have national or international importance. Though the foundations must be the same, the foundation should be built in accordance to God's specific direction, discernment of the particular dangers (conflicts) of the surrounding environment, and local resources.

Light and Lenses

The light room is bounded by glass windows that extend from floor to ceiling, with the illuminant is placed centrally. Many lighthouses use lenses invented in 1822 by Augustin-Jean Fresnel. His invention maximized the weak oil-light sources of the day, enabling the light to be seen as far as twenty miles out to sea. Some of these lenses are 12 feet tall and 6 feet in diameter. Fresnel's design consists of a central lens in the middle of several concentric circular prisms. Hundreds of triangular prisms placed at the top and bottom of the concentric rings catch the light radiated outward by the illuminant, and refract or bend it toward the beam. Fresnel achieved a 70 percent capture of the available light, which became focused into a pencil beam. Fresnel's lenses, which can weigh up to five tons, are rotated by clocklike mechanisms and float over beds of mercury or roll almost effortlessly on bearings referred to as "chariot wheels."

Selahs are like Fresnel's lenses. They are designed by God to maximize the available light source. With much less light and fuel, selahs can create a single powerful beam that can be seen for miles. Yielding to God's prescription for acceptable worship allows the worshiper to expend much less energy and obtain quicker entrance to the heavenlies.

Summary

The recent development of 24-hour ministries across the globe signals the coming restoration of biblical worship. The desire to offer the "acceptable worship" is growing more and more in the hearts of musicians and intercessors. Worshipers are becoming more aware of the awesome power available through selahs as established in Davidic worship.

The mystique of the lighthouse, as a place of great beauty, serenity, and adventure, is slowly finding a place in the church. As lighthouses spring up, let the builders seek wisdom in its design and construction.

The information presented on lighthouses is taken from *Anatomy of the Lighthouse* by Michael J. Rhein. The information on biblical worship and selahs is taken from Ray Hughes' *The Minstrel Series* tapes. ■

It is well for us to remember that Jesus had scorching words of rebuke in His day for those who were able by the skies to read the coming storms and yet were blind to the signs of the times.
Can we read the signs of our times?

—Leonard Ravenhill

≫≫ Mustard Seeds of Wisdom ≪≪

WHEN God WALKED THE EARTH
Part III

by Rick Joyner

Michael, the angelic captains, and their hosts continued gazing at the terrible spectacle before them. The wilderness had been overshadowed by the cloud of demons that had lasted for almost forty days now, since the Son had entered for His confrontation with Lucifer. Not since the rebellion in heaven had the two hosts faced each other like this. For forty days the evil horde of demons hurled insults and feigned attacks at the angelic army, which they knew were under strict orders not to respond.

Michael and his captains had watched helplessly as the evil horde had assaulted the population of Israel. They gathered into storms to send hail to destroy their crops. They mercilessly blew trees over into dwellings and struck people with lightning as if it were a great game to them. They afflicted men, women, and children with every kind of disease. They even agitated the Roman troops to mischief and sowed bitterness and rebellion in everyone's heart in which they found an opening.

Through all of this the evil horde had but one goal—to get the Son to respond in His authority as God. They did not understand it, but their master, Lucifer himself, had said that they were doomed if Jesus did not abandon His manhood and respond to them in His power as God. They had to provoke Him to do something that the Father had not sent Him to do.

Lucifer himself looked down upon the spectacle. With his legions darkening the sky, he was feeling more and more confident. He looked at the angelic hosts standing passively and felt nothing but contempt. He turned to his lieutenants and sweeping his hand across the horizon where the angelic host stood, he said,

"They will soon be ours! I am about to induce their Master to serve me, and then they will serve us also. This is the moment we have been waiting for! This is even better than when I seduced Adam and Eve—much better! How foolish for the Father to deliver the Son into my hands like this! He even sent Him in the form of man, the weakest of all creatures at resisting me! You will soon witness my greatest triumph. We will celebrate by destroying this pitiful little people, the Jews that He, for some inexplicable reason, has cared so much about."

Jesus sat on the hillside looking out over the wilderness. He longed for fellowship with His Father again. He knew that the Father was beholding Him, and He knew that the Holy Spirit was with Him, but He longed to behold the Father and to feel the Holy Spirit again. Now He felt so weak. For the first time in weeks, hunger was coming upon Him in waves and the cold seemed to grip the very marrow of His bones. This body of flesh had become more of a burden than He had ever known before. How He longed to be free of it!

He began looking at the stones. They almost looked like bread. How easy it would be to turn one of them into a loaf and satisfy this terrible pain! Quickly He caught Himself, turning away from the stones to look out over the countryside.

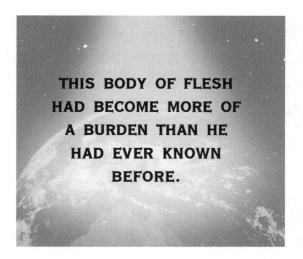

THIS BODY OF FLESH HAD BECOME MORE OF A BURDEN THAN HE HAD EVER KNOWN BEFORE.

Then depression swept over Him like the waves of hunger had before. How dreary this world was! How He longed to see the Father's glory again. How tired He was of seeing the continual selfishness in the hearts of men. Everyone only sought their own good and cared only for themselves. If He were a king now He could show them the evil of their ways! But wasn't that what so many other kings had tried to do, only to be reduced to an even more terrible selfishness? Then He would be no different from them, He mused. He stood up and looked around. Where were these thoughts coming from?

"I must not continue to let My mind drift like this," He thought to Himself. "I'm the Son of God. I not only dwell in the glory, I have the glory within Me. I have the power. I could even move the mountains if I wished. I could dispel this dreary weather with the lifting of My finger."

Lucifer saw his chance. The weakness of Jesus' flesh had now made Him vulnerable. He was tottering on the edge. Now He could be pressed into using His power for His own selfish reasons.

"And He thought that He would condemn me for using the power for myself, and seeking glory for myself. He is about to show that He is just like me!" Satan whispered to his commanders as he left them.

JESUS HAD AGAIN KNELT TO PRAY, MOSTLY TO BATTLE THE THOUGHTS THAT WERE NOW SEEMINGLY BOMBARDING HIM THROUGH THE RAIN ITSELF.

As Satan lifted up, the evil horde stopped swirling and almost in unison gasped with a confusing combination of both ecstasy and fear. Wind swept across the mountains so that the rain was driven before it in sheets. Satan turned and thrust his hand in the air as if directing his legions to back off. He despised these whining little creatures and demons almost as much as they feared him. He directed his commanders to control them so that they would again form a cloud of depression over the area. He then proceeded toward the Son, almost gleeful with anticipation.

Jesus had again knelt to pray, mostly to battle the thoughts that were now seemingly bombarding Him through the rain itself. Sensing the presence behind Him, He turned and looked up at Lucifer.

Lucifer stood in his most glorious apparel, more stunning than any Caesar had ever imagined. His face was so kindly and appealing that any child would have easily come to him. Jesus knew him immediately and slowly stood to His feet to face him.

"I am very sorry to see You like this," Lucifer offered, giving a slight bow. "We have had our differences, but this is quite shocking. You are after all the Son of God Who made me. Is there something I can do for You?" Then after a pause, he continued, "Of course, You, being the Son, do not need for me to do anything for You. I will be glad to turn the stones into bread for You, but I'm sure You can still do that much."

Jesus looked at Lucifer. He looked more regal than the angelic captains. His face was more kindly than he had ever seen on a man. His voice was more soothing and compelling than He had heard since coming to earth. This was the voice that Eve had heard. He watched as Lucifer picked up a stone that in fact looked like a loaf of bread.

"Dear Jesus—that is what You want me to call You now, isn't it? Please, turn this into bread. You deserve this after all You have been through. You need Your strength. Then we can talk. Of course, I will be glad to do it for You if You can't."

For a moment Jesus thought He could smell the bread. Never had He thought that anything on this earth could be so appealing. He took it out of Lucifer's hand. He held it, looked at it, and surprisingly, smelled the bread again, faintly. It aroused His hunger like He had never experienced before.

"I have never desired bread like this before," Jesus admitted. "But My Father made this to be a stone, and He has not shown Me that I am to turn His stones into bread. He loves Me more than the birds of the air and He feeds them every day. So if He has not chosen to feed Me today, it is for My good because He loves Me. I only want to eat what My Father provides for Me. **Man shall not live by bread alone, but by every word that proceeds from the mouth of God" (Matthew 4:4 NKJV)**, Jesus responded, looking up at Lucifer.

"Of course," the devil responded, not changing his demeanor or showing anything but his seeming concern. "So, the Father has stripped You of Your powers as well. Why would He do that if He trusted You?"

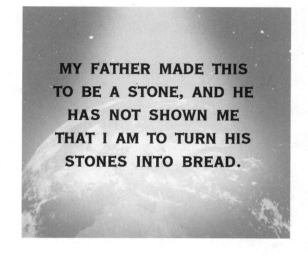

MY FATHER MADE THIS TO BE A STONE, AND HE HAS NOT SHOWN ME THAT I AM TO TURN HIS STONES INTO BREAD.

Instantly, Jesus and the devil were standing on the pinnacle of the temple.

"Listen, I am only doing this to help You. It looks like the Father has betrayed You just like He did me. If You are still His Son, if He has not disowned You, which it sure seems to me that He must have done, cast Yourself off of this temple and see if He rescues You."

Jesus looked down, feeling faint from the lack of food. Something in Him wanted to jump just to feel the Father's love for Him again. Satan continued:

"Do the Scriptures not say, **'He shall give his angels charge over you,'** and **'In their hands they shall bear you up lest you dash Your foot against a stone'"** (Matthew 4:6 NKJV). Surely then He will send His angels to catch

You if You were to jump off of this temple. That is, if He still considers You His Son. If He doesn't, You will know that He has done all of this to You just to destroy You. Then You will know that You are being cast away just as I was. I know You do not want to use Your powers for Yourself, but if He does not send His angels to save You, then You had better learn to use them for Yourself, just like I did, and this is as good a time as any to find out."

> TO DOUBT HIS FAITHFULNESS WOULD BE TO DOUBT THE POWER THAT UPHOLDS THE UNIVERSE, WHICH GAVE LIFE TO MEN AND ANGELS.

Weakness was now sweeping over Jesus in waves like the hunger was earlier. Never had he felt this bad. How He longed to see the Father or feel the Holy Spirit. How great it would be to just see an angel. He looked at the temple, where He had enjoyed so much sweet fellowship with the Father. He remembered conversing about the Scriptures with the elders when He was young, and what a delight it was to learn them, ponder them, and see them from man's perspective.

No! He could not test the Father the way men were constantly doing. To doubt His faithfulness would be to doubt the power that upholds the universe, which gave life to men and angels. This was the doubt that Eve allowed to take root in her soul. The serpent has not changed his ways at all.

"You shall not test the Lord your God," Jesus responded.

"Very well. I understand," Lucifer offered, in his most humble and compassionate voice. "It is just hard for me to understand why You are in such a state. But You are right. You know that You are the Son and You do not need to prove that."

"I must apologize for these uncontrollable demon hordes," Lucifer remarked as he turned to look at the chaos they were creating. "They are perpetually hungry, almost as much as You are. They must feed their appetites or they really get out of control. Since the curse upon us is that we must eat the dust, which You used to make the flesh of man, our only food here is the flesh of men. We, therefore, must satisfy ourselves with man's passions. The more we can inflame them, the more we ourselves are filled. Of course, men invite us to do that by turning from the Words that proceed from the mouth of God and seeking their fulfillment through the lusts of the flesh. So we are feeding each other. But it is a pitiful existence for both of us," Lucifer said, turning to look at Jesus.

"Do you see those demons of lust out there?" Satan almost whispered. "Since I made them leave the orgies in Rome and come here, they are nearly starving. Many of the people here have learned to feed on the Word of God. Many of the rest have learned to keep their passions in check with all of their traditions. But those lust demons are not as stupid as they appear. They can unravel those traditions and even use them to sow more lust in their hearts. These men become even more devoted to appearing pious on the outside in order to cover up the corruption in their hearts. The demons don't really care. As long as they can cause the lust to grow in their hearts, their appetite is satisfied."

Lucifer watched the grief rise in Jesus' eyes. The Son of God mourned deeply as He thought of the spiritual and moral corruption of His own Father's bride, and His mother, the nation of Israel. The devil then continued,

"You have probably witnessed how the lust that is now in some of the most pious appearing men here is much greater than we have ever seen in Rome. Of course, the demons of deception and the religious demons, like this even more. Most of them have decided that they really do not want to return to Rome because they have it so good here. I think it will now only be a short time before they have seduced even those who really love the Word of God."

THE SON OF GOD MOURNED DEEPLY AS HE THOUGHT OF THE SPIRITUAL AND MORAL CORRUPTION OF HIS OWN FATHER'S BRIDE, AND HIS MOTHER, THE NATION OF ISRAEL.

Lucifer again looked at Jesus, Who was grieved to the point of tears which streamed down His face. The devil patiently let it all sink in, and then continued.

"It seems that very soon this whole nation will be bowing down to me, just like the Romans and the Greeks before them. Of course, I will not bring the idols back. I must confess that what You did through the Maccabees has made that difficult here. Even so, this only caused those religious demons to show some creativity. Now they have learned how to get men to even make an idol out of the Scriptures, their traditions, and of course, their own high religious titles and positions. The High Priest is now far more adored here than Your Father. Now they even esteem and trust the Pharisees more than Him, and the Pharisees love their leaders more than Him."

> "...LOOK HOW THEY ACTUALLY ENJOY THE COMPANY OF MY DEMONS MORE THAN THEY WANT TO BE WITH YOU OR YOUR FATHER."

Lucifer again turned to look at Jesus, who remained silent, but was grieving more and more.

"I really don't care to do this to these pitiful little people. I personally enjoy it much more in Rome now. But with You here, we now have to concentrate our efforts. If You are going to try to lead them back to obedience, I must do all that I can to stop You. We are having so much success now that it will only be a matter of time before we have completely destroyed these people. That would be a pity. I really do not get any pleasure out of that. I do not know why You love them so much or why You care so much for men

at all, but we do enjoy them for entertainment and they are the only food we have now.

"And look how they actually enjoy the company of my demons more than they want to be with You or Your Father. They are very soon about to destroy themselves with their self-centeredness and neither of us want that. I have thought of a solution that may work for all of us."

Lucifer again turned and looked at Jesus with what seemed to be the most genuine compassion. Pausing for just a few seconds, he continued in a slightly lower voice.

"I know You love these people, and I know You want to help them. I do not care to go on destroying them like this. In fact, I, too, would rather be rid of these lowly demons and their sick perversions. This world is now mine. Adam gave it to me when he chose to serve me. At first I was just angry at God for banishing me from heaven. That is why I released all of these hordes with their perversions and diseases, but now I just want to exist in peace. If You will just acknowledge me as the lord here, I will let You rule over all of the kingdoms of this world. Then You can have them all living under that Law You gave to Moses. You can make them righteous, and give them peace and joy. You would make a wonderful ruler in this realm! Do it for them."

Then Lucifer pointed at the evil horde that was darkening the sky.

"Then You can send all of these hordes to the pit, and I, too, will be glad to see them go. Then there will be no more wars or diseases and men will begin to live as long as Adam again, a thousand years, or even longer if You will lift that ban and let them find the Tree of Life again. Then there will be peace on earth. I will let You do whatever You want. All You have to do is take one bow before me to acknowledge my legal right, so I know that the Father will not banish me from here as He did from heaven.

Jesus was looking intently at Lucifer. "I have Him right on the brink," the devil thought to himself. He waited to be sure that his next statement would hit with its maximum impact, pushing Him over the edge into the trap.

As Lucifer watched the compassion he saw in Jesus for those poor people, it was even greater than he had thought. "How weak that compassion is making Him," the devil pondered. "I must resolve to never let it get even the smallest grip on me. It is an enemy of all true strength."

Even so, the devil was the master at feigning compassion. It seemed to be working on Jesus like his other schemes had not. "False compassion is as strong as vengeance, if used properly," he thought, straining to hide the contempt he badly wanted to show for the Son who had allowed Himself to fall to such a state of weakness in that frail human body. Gathering himself, Lucifer then offered what he knew would be the clincher.

> "FALSE COMPASSION IS AS STRONG AS VENGEANCE, IF USED PROPERLY," HE THOUGHT, STRAINING TO HIDE THE CONTEMPT HE BADLY WANTED TO SHOW FOR THE SON...

"I know Your body is hurting You now. I do not know how You have endured being in it for so long. And to think that the Father wants You to endure several more years of it! But what I really do not understand, is how, if He really loved You, could He possibly ask You, the Son of God, the Lord of glory, to endure the shame and torture of that cross! What could possibly be the reason for that? And for these pitiful little creatures? How could that possibly help them?"

After letting that sink in, he continued, "It was that reasoning which caused me to turn against Him when I did. I remember Your glory. I cannot even bear to see You like this, much less on a cross! Just take one little bow to me and You can avoid all of that and return to Your glorious state immediately. It will be so easy and so quick. Just do it, and then we can return this universe to some sanity."

Lucifer put on his best face of compassion. "Please. Let's just do it and get it over with," he entreated.

> EVERY ANGEL IN THE REGION SAW WHAT WAS HAPPENING AND THE PRAISES OF GOD AND HIS SON QUICKLY ROSE ABOVE THE TUMULT OF THE FLEEING DEMONS.

Then he waited, sure that Jesus would bow at any moment. He studied Jesus' face, looking for any sign of His submission, but became concerned when the compassion on His face did not change. Finally, Jesus turned and looked resolutely into the face of Lucifer.

"Depart from Me, Satan! The Scriptures say that 'You shall do homage to the Lord God, and Him only shall you worship'" (see Matthew 4:10).

The smug arrogance turned quickly to terror as Satan retreated in haste. He knew that the Son had the power to destroy him with a word or even a gesture. The fear that overwhelmed him quickly spread throughout the demonic hordes. They fled in every direction, as their terrified curses filled the air. Every angel in the region saw what was happening and the praises of God and His Son quickly rose above the tumult of the fleeing demons.

Michael and the captains, who had been standing with him in their long and trying vigil, now rushed to the Son.

"Lord. We thank the Father that You endured this terrible trial," Michael said, as soon as they reached Him. "It was a terrible trial for us as well, watching You endure that onslaught of evil. We could not even see through the demonic cloud what was happening, but we could feel it. This whole part of the world could feel it. But thank the Father that You are alright! He instructed us to give You this bread and to tell You how pleased He is with You."

At those words the eyes of Jesus glistened, and He stood to His feet with a strength that He had not felt for many days. Lifting His hands to heaven He cried out in great joy,

"Father, I am well pleased with You. All of Your ways are perfect. Thank You for My strength. Thank You for Your Holy Spirit. Thank

You for this bread, but even more, thank You for Your love and grace."

With that, Jesus sat back on a stone and began to eat His bread.

"My friends," He said, looking up at Michael and the captains, "Such bread is a simple but great pleasure, which I have come to greatly appreciate as a man, but never as much as I do this loaf today. And after forty days of seeing nothing but that evil cloud, I am just as thankful to see your faces."

"Lord, we are glad that we bring joy to You. This time has been most difficult for all of us. We were all subject to Lucifer's guile when he tried to persuade us to rebel with him in heaven. We were in heaven, beholding the glory and majesty of the Father all around us, and it was still convincing, as many of our fellows succumbed to it. Adam and Eve succumbed to it even while they were dwelling in the Paradise, with the Father's goodness all around them. It will forever be a marvel for all of creation that You resisted him in such a weakened state, in the midst of such a wicked and evil world, even under such a cloud of depression! If any ever doubted that You were worthy of Your position, I do not think that they do now."

As Michael looked at the Son, he marveled at Him even more than he did when He had agreed to become a man and dwell on the earth among them. To all angels this had been incomprehensible, but for Him to endure the kind of temptation He had just suffered, this would cause all of the angels to marvel for many ages to come.

> AS MICHAEL LOOKED AT THE SON, HE MARVELED AT HIM EVEN MORE THAN HE DID WHEN HE HAD AGREED TO BECOME A MAN AND DWELL ON THE EARTH AMONG THEM.

"Forgive me," Michael continued, "But You look very bad right now in body, even if in Your heart there is none like You. This is truly a day of glory and victory in which we will forever rejoice. You have defeated the devil...even in the form of a man! The joy of Your Father and the joy in heaven has not been this great since we all sang together and the worlds came into being."

As Jesus stood, the sky for a thousand miles in every direction glistened with the swords of the angelic hosts that were drawn in a salute to Him. In heaven the glory of the celebration was greater than had ever been witnessed before. Every angel, every cherubim, and every created being in heaven, sang, danced, and rejoiced with all that was within them. New colors were born as the Father's delight overflowed to embrace the great hosts of angels and beings that He loved so much, which He and His Son had brought forth together.

Soon man, who had fallen to the depths of depravity and darkness, would be assured of one day beholding this glory, too. They were even now assured of one day beholding the greatest glory of all, because they would rise from the greatest darkness. This was the greatest delight of the Father, to share beauty and glory with those who could see it, because all beauty and glory were the result of His love, and He longed for those He could share His love with.

> THERE WOULD NEVER AGAIN BE A DOUBT THAT THE KING IN HIS GREATEST WEAKNESS WAS STILL MUCH STRONGER THAN THE EVIL ONE IN HIS GREATEST STRENGTH.

As Jesus began to walk along the dusty road from the wilderness, He could feel the delight of the Father. All of the angels who lined the road, swords drawn in salute as they bowed on one knee, could also feel His delight. Hours before it had been the darkest of times, and now it

was the brightest. How quickly it had all changed!

The entire host that was with Michael and his commanders all knew that the heavens were filled with the highest worship, but not one would now trade his place on the earth for what was happening in heaven. There would never again be a doubt that the King in His greatest weakness was still much stronger than the evil one in his greatest strength.

Michael turned to his commanders, saying "There will never again be a doubt in the creation that the Lord will forever be triumphant. Truth will forever prevail over every lie of the devil. The lies and deception of the father of lies has now been made manifest. The "last Adam" had prevailed where the first had failed. Now the glorious victory was certain."

Simon and Andrew were weary. They had fished all night without catching even enough for their breakfast. Andrew was just as weary of hearing Simon complain and even chide him about his belief that Jesus was the Messiah. Andrew had to admit though, that he had even begun to have doubts. Neither did it seem that he would be returning for him as He had promised.

It had now been many weeks, and not only had Jesus not returned, there had been no news of Him. After the great expectations that had arisen because of the Baptist, there now seemed to be a great pall of depression over the whole land. Not only had the skies been darkened by clouds for days, but great storms had whipped the land like a scourge. It was almost as if Jehovah had forsaken them altogether. Andrew now felt that the darkness in his heart was as great as the darkness over the land. It did seem as if Jesus had just disappeared.

The argument between the two brothers over the work that needed to be done to secure the boat was rising to a crescendo when they heard a great commotion coming from the town. They both stopped to look as it became louder, and was obviously coming their way. It sounded like a wedding celebration, but it was much too early for that. As a young boy came around the corner, they called to him, "What is this about, young man?"

"Jesus is here! The One who has been healing the sick has come to us!"

Simon and Andrew looked at each other. Finally Simon asked, "What does he mean by 'the One who heals the sick?'"

"I do not know. I guess we have been out so long that we have missed the news that the others have heard. But at least He has come!"

At that time the whole crowd came around the corner, with Jesus walking in the front. Without hesitation He came right up to Andrew and Simon, stepped down into their boat, and asked them to

cast off. Peter hesitated, scowled, and then pushed off.

They had not gone far, when Jesus raised His hand for them to stop. He then began to speak to the crowd, which had by now spread out all along the docks and seemed to fill every available place.

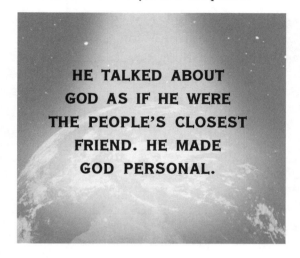

HE TALKED ABOUT GOD AS IF HE WERE THE PEOPLE'S CLOSEST FRIEND. HE MADE GOD PERSONAL.

As Jesus taught the people, Andrew and Simon sat in the back of the boat and watched with amazement. His words flowed over the great crowd like a gentle breeze. It settled them and gave them hope. He talked about God as if He were the people's closest friend. He made God personal. He made them feel like God was right there with them.

After about an hour, Jesus told the people to go to their homes, to enjoy each other, and rest. They did not want to go, but they began to depart, while there was such rejoicing that Peter wondered if he had ever seen a group of people so happy. A half dozen songs broke out from different groups as they walked along, and from the boat they seemed to form a harmony.

Simon and Andrew sat speechless as the Lord turned to them, "Put out into the deep water and let down your nets."

After a moment Simon replied, "Sir, we have fished all night and have caught nothing." Jesus did not say anything. Finally, after a few minutes, Simon offered, "At Your bidding we will try again."

"Right here will be fine," Jesus said.

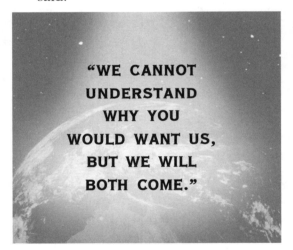

"WE CANNOT UNDERSTAND WHY YOU WOULD WANT US, BUT WE WILL BOTH COME."

Andrew and Simon let the nets down. As soon as they hit the water, the nets were filled with more fish than they had ever caught before. Soon the nets even began to break. Seeing their neighbors nearby, Simon waved to them to come help. Jesus just sat looking on as they filled both boats with the great quantity of fish.

When they had finished, Simon and Andrew sat down and looked at Jesus. Immediately, Simon remembered what he had said to Andrew when he told him about Jesus, and how he believed that He was the Messiah. Simon had ridiculed him, saying that he was glad that the Messiah was coming back for him and that maybe He could tell them where the fish were.

Andrew was thinking about the same conversation, and about how he had replied that this was expecting too much of the Messiah, that only God could do that.

Both Andrew and Simon looked down at all of the fish, then at each other. They looked over at the other boats that were also struggling to haul in the great load of fish. They then looked up at Jesus, and He was looking at them. He looked at Simon with such a knowing look that he was sure he knew of that conversation. A great fear gripped Simon as he fell to his knees.

"Please Sir! Depart from me. I am such a sinner. I am not worthy for You to be in my boat."

"I am not here because you are worthy," Jesus replied. "I am here for Andrew and for you. Will you come?"

Simon began to weep uncontrollably. Andrew put his arms around him and turned to Jesus.

"We cannot understand why You would want us, but we will both come."

The three walked in silence until they came upon Zebedee and his sons. They were sitting in their boat, mending nets. James and his father had tried for days to console John, but John was nearly distraught. He had been sure that Jesus would return for him, but now it had been many weeks. He just could not consider that they had been wrong about Jesus. The Baptist had been so sure. They had heard the voice like thunder with their own ears, but now it all seemed so far away, so obscure.

"Father," John replied, "I just cannot get interested in anything but God. I have seen too much after being with the Baptist for so long. God is moving on our people. Our land is alive again with the sense of His presence. How can I think about business? I do not know why Jesus did not return for me, but I just cannot give up. I must now go and find Him. I would rather starve looking for the Messiah than live in luxury without Him. I know that this Jesus is the Messiah. I just cannot believe otherwise."

"Yes, my son," Zebedee replied, "but if He is the Messiah, He must be a man of truth, and He gave you His word that He would return for you. If He does not keep His word to you, He is not the One. You cannot compromise that either."

John just slumped over. He knew what his father said was true. That God's Word was true was the foundation of their faith. How could anyone be a true representative of the Lord if he did not keep his word? Despair rolled over John like a blanket. His hopes had been so high. Now he was equally low.

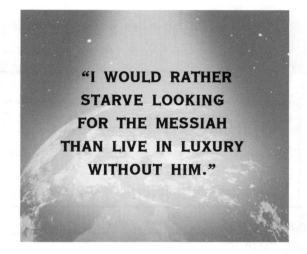

"I WOULD RATHER STARVE LOOKING FOR THE MESSIAH THAN LIVE IN LUXURY WITHOUT HIM."

"Peace, My friends," a voice said behind them.

John spun around so fast that his father and brother were almost knocked off the boat. They all three then stood. Jesus was standing on the shore.

"I will never leave you nor forsake you. I also know that you will never leave Me. Come, for it is time for the journey to begin."

John was now almost numb with joy. Large tears rolled down his cheeks. He bowed low, and then exclaimed,

"Father, brother. He is here! This is Jesus, the One for whom I have waited."

"You have waited for Me for a few weeks, but I have waited for you even longer. Now let us be about My Father's business." ■

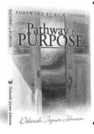

MORNINGSTAR | *School of Ministry*
Ephesians 4:1 Live Worthy of the Calling

MSM is a one or two year curriculum, depending on your needs and experience. Graduates of the first year curriculum can go on to an internship program with the MorningStar leadership team.

The MSM curriculum is intended to raise up a new generation of radical Christian leaders who are committed to sound biblical truth, to be like Christ, do the works that He did, and never retreat before the enemies of the cross.

Housing available for 2005-2006 term.

MorningStar School of Ministry has been approved by the president of the University of North Carolina and the UNC Board of Governors to offer an Associate Degree in Christian Ministry.

For more information or to request an application call 803-547-9655 or write to MSM, P.O. Box 19409, Charlotte NC 28219

This school is authorized under Federal law to enroll non-immigrant students.

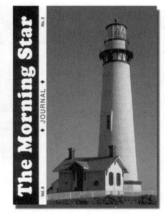

MorningStar Strategic Team

MST FINANCES

MST IS
our partners' fellowship – those united with us in prayer and support of our strategic missions.

are invested in missions of strategic importance, such as the restoration of H.I.M. and the equipping and sending out of powerful and effective missions.

MEMBERS CONTRIBUTE
$15.00 per month, $150 per year, or more.

JOIN THE TEAM

Please send completed form to:
MorningStar P.O. Box 440, Wilkesboro, NC 28697
Fax: 1-336-651-2430

Contact MST:
1-800-542-0278
mst@morningstarministries.org

Name _____ Date _____

Address _____

City _____ State _____ Zip _____

( ) _____
Phone   E-mail

Here is my contribution of $_____ to MST in the form of:

☐ Cash   ☐ Check   ☐ Money Order (payable to MST)   ☐ Credit Card

MSJ0605

Charge my:
☐ Master Card
☐ Visa
☐ Discover
☐ AMEX

Credit Card
☐☐☐☐ ☐☐☐☐ ☐☐☐☐ ☐☐☐☐

Expiration Date
☐☐ / ☐☐

Signature: _____ (Credit Card contributions will not be processed without a signature)

☐ Please automatically deduct $_____ from the above credit card each month.
Deducted the first business week of each month. Though we do not encourage debt, automatic deduction is a reliable method of supporting ministries conveniently. You may cancel at any time.

Note: MorningStar will never sell or give away your personal information. If for any reason you would like to stop deductions from your credit card or withdraw from MST, you can call 1-800-542-0278.

Join Us in a Historic Restoration

MorningStar purchased the former Heritage USA Grand Hotel and Conference Center, along with fifty-two acres of property, and established Heritage International Ministries (H.I.M.).

HOTEL ROOM
AT H.I.M.

THE NEHEMIAH PROJECT
RESTORE A HOTEL ROOM

You, your family, church, business, or group can restore a hotel room at H.I.M. Each room you help to restore will be named in your honor or as a memorial to the one you choose.

For more information, visit the H.I.M. section of www.morningstarministries.org. You can also contact Tiffany Taylor at HIM@morningstarministries.org or by calling 336-651-2400, ext. 113.

TAKE A SECTION OF THE WALL

Please send completed form to: The Nehemiah Project, P.O. Box 440, Wilkesboro, NC 28697

☐ **$5,000 to restore a hotel room**
For each $5,000 a room will be named in your honor.
(You can pay installments of $500/month)

☐ **$1,000 or more**
For $1000 or more your name will be placed on our Nehemiah's wall.
(You can pay installments of $100/month)

☐ **Any size donation**
Your name will be placed on the Permanent Register.

Name _____ Date _____

Address _____

City _____ State _____ Zip _____

(_____) _____
Phone _____ E-mail _____

Here is my contribution of $_____ in the form of ☐ Cash ☐ Check ☐ Money Order ☐ CreditCard

Charge my:
☐ Master Card
☐ Visa
☐ Discover
☐ AMEX

Credit Card
☐☐☐☐ ☐☐☐☐ ☐☐☐☐ ☐☐☐☐

Expiration Date MSJ0605
☐☐ / ☐☐

Signature: _____ (Credit Card contributions will not be processed without a signature)

☐ Please automatically deduct $_____ from the above credit card each month.
Deducted the first business week of each month. Though we do not encourage debt, automatic deduction is a reliable method of supporting ministries conveniently. You may cancel at any time.

Note: MorningStar will never sell or give away your personal information. If for any reason you would like to stop deductions from your credit card, please call 1-800-542-0278.